Keeping it Together

A guide for support staff working with
people whose behaviour is challenging

Peter Woodward, Steve Hardy and Theresa Joyce

estia centre

Keeping it Together

A guide for support staff working with people whose behaviour is challenging

© Peter Woodward, Steve Hardy and Theresa Joyce

The authors have asserted their rights in accordance with the *Copyright, Designs and Patents Act 1988* to be identified as the authors of this work.

Published by:

Pavilion Publishing (Brighton) Ltd
Richmond House
Richmond Road
Brighton BN2 3RL

Tel: 01273 623222
Fax: 01273 625526
Email: info@pavpub.com
Web: www.pavpub.com

First published 2007

A Catalogue record for this book is available from the British Library.

ISBN-13: 978 1 84196 189 7
ISBN-10: 1 84196 189 2

Editor: Grace Fairley (www.thebigwideword.com)
Cover design: Tony Pitt
Page layout: Jigsaw Design
Printing: Hobbs the Printers Limited (Hampshire)

Contents

About the authors

Peter Woodward

Peter Woodward is a Registered Nurse in Learning Disabilities and has worked in forensic and assessment and treatment services for people with learning disabilities and challenging behaviour. At the time of writing this guide, Peter was employed as Training Officer at the Estia Centre. He is now a Senior Lecturer at the University of Greenwich.

Steve Hardy

Steve Hardy is the Training and Consultancy Manager at the Estia Centre. Steve is a Registered Nurse in Learning Disabilities. He has worked in a variety of services for people with challenging behaviour and mental health needs, including residential, day services and secure environments. His interests include mental health promotion, involving people that use services, staff training and accessible information for people with learning disabilities.

Theresa Joyce

Dr Theresa Joyce is Consultant Clinical Psychologist and Head of Psychology and Behavioural Support Services at the South London and Maudsley NHS Foundation Trust. She has extensive experience in working with staff in residential services, including those supporting people with complex challenging behaviours. She has also designed and delivered training on working with people with challenging behaviour, including the modules on challenging behaviour in the *Mental Health in Learning Disabilities* Training Pack (2005).

The Estia Centre

The Estia Centre is a training, research and development resource for those who support adults with learning disabilities with additional mental health needs and challenging behaviour. The Estia Centre is based on the Guy's Hospital Campus and is an integral part of local services for people with learning disabilities provided by the South London & Maudsley NHS Trust. The Estia Centre is also an Academic Section of the Institute of Psychiatry of (Division of Psychological Medicine and Health Service Research Department) King's College London.

Acknowledgements

The authors would like to thank the following people for their guidance and support in producing this guide:

Choice Support

Helen Adeleke
Ruth Agboola
William Awopejy
Nancy Bangara
Daphne Banton
Pauline Bryan
Evelyn Carter
Yinka Coker
Paula Dalphinis
Tracy Eastlake
Desmond Francis
Emmanuel Hanson
Ron Hurley
Gaber Kaffel
Bola Lowal
David Mukasa
Clarissa McKriete
Annette Naddainba
Ola Omokioe
Yeda Williams

Lewisham Social Services

Vicky McLeod
Bill Lord
Gail Rigby
Matt Marshall
Junior Calder
Cynthia Cunningham
Annette McLaughlin
Angela Pinnock

South London & Maudsley NHS Trust

Chris Brennan
Ben Burk
Jim Molloy
Ray Nambiar
Gervase Newrick
Alf Owen
Anne Parris

Oxleas NHS Trust

Sam Allen
Joyce Broom
Shelley Burroughs
Emma Corrie
Lorraine Dance
Kate Dunn
John Holding
Margaret Larkin
Colette Meehen
Colin Miller
Tim Mitchell
Tracy Owen

Three Cs, Lewisham

Joseph Alozie
Patricia Dawes
Janet Dennis
Ivy Lewis
Angela Lovell
Selma Martin
Rachel Ohusiem
Henry Rhima
Lena Sobatie
Mitzie Stephenson
Jan Underhill

Providence Project, Lewisham

Ron Dempster
Aurora Charity
Naaz Manji

Lewisham Partnership

Theresa Foley
Richard Lovegrove

Lambeth Mencap

Christina Bing
Minevver Borova
Desiree Forte-Burnett
Yoke Hopkins
Agnes Huston
Sharon Jones
Daisy Keleva
Samantha Low
Flo MacCrimmon
Valerie Madden
Ester Potman
Jenny Runnicles
Jacqueline Smith
Lesley Wickens

Speaking Up Southwark

(13 members participated; only the following wanted their names included)

Lara Akinfadni
Rebecca Haines
Linda West
Paul Boyle
Roger Brooksby

About this guide

This guide is designed for support staff working with people with learning disabilities, who are new to challenging behaviour or facing challenging behaviour for the first time.

The guide came about for a number of reasons. Although there are many books available on challenging behaviour, few are specifically aimed at support staff or those facing challenging behaviour for the first time.

This guide has been written in plain English so that it is easier to understand. The use of psychological terms has been avoided.

It is a practical guide offering solutions that staff with no previous experience in this field can use.

The authors consulted many people working within learning disabilities services, including residential home support workers and managers, day service support staff and practitioners from challenging needs teams. People with learning disabilities were also consulted and asked for their opinions, which make up a valuable contribution to this guide.

Finally, the authors would like to thank all those who assisted in writing this guide. Their help was much appreciated.

section one

Facing challenging behaviour for the first time

This section covers:

- what you should do if you are new to a service and have not worked with people whose behaviour is challenging before

- what you should do if you already work in a service and the behaviour of a person you support has just become challenging for the first time.

How does challenging behaviour make people feel?

Challenging behaviour is a subject that most people have an opinion about, and it makes people have many different feelings. You may have believed that you failed, or you may have felt guilty about your experiences. Here's what some support workers said:

What to do when starting work in a new service

Starting work in a service such as a supported house, outreach team or day service can be an anxious time; there are new people to get to know – people that use the service, and staff – a new manager, and new routines and ways of working. It can be even more anxiety-provoking if the people who use the service have behaviour we find challenging. Here are some tips on how to build your confidence.

Read the guidelines

Most people whose behaviour is challenging will have some kind of guidelines (these may be called care plans or care programmes). These should include what to do when the person's behaviour becomes challenging. They should also inform you of the possible 'triggers' for the challenging behaviour and how these can be avoided. Triggers are the things that make the behaviour happen. There should also be guidelines that aren't just about reacting to a challenging situation, but will give you some ideas of how to make the person's quality of life better. They might tell you how to involve the person in a range of activities they enjoy or how to effectively communicate with the individual. If someone's quality of life is improved, then the challenging behaviour should happen less often.

Observe experienced staff

It is normal practice for new staff to have a period of being supernumerary (not being counted in the staff numbers). Make sure that you spend this time with experienced members of staff **who follow the existing guidelines**. Watch how they interact with the people who use the service, the language they use, how they engage them in activities and how they deal with difficult situations. It is important that the staff are following the existing guidelines and that, when you develop your own ways of working with the people who use the service, you follow them too.

Consistency

It is important that every member of staff works with the person in the same way. We call this having a consistent approach. Any care plan or intervention will only work if all the staff are doing it. If not all staff are working in the same way, the individual will get mixed messages (see the example in *Box 1: Mandy*).

Box 1: Mandy

Mandy attends a day service, where the staff have found her behaviour a challenge. There appear to be problems around Mandy being able to make her needs known. She will grab at staff and attempt to drag them to what she wants, often when they are not able to accompany her.

The team of eight staff has been working closely with members of the community learning disability team and a plan has been drawn up that supports Mandy to request items using objects. Mandy now carries a bag with different objects in it and can request a drink by showing a cup or ask to go shopping by showing a photo of the local shops.

At first, the staff had to prompt Mandy by showing her the object associated to whatever activity or item Mandy had led them to. The first week was not that successful but by the second week, all of the staff were working the same way and Mandy began to realise that the items were associated with what she wanted. She realised that she could use the objects instead of dragging members of staff to where she wanted them.

One member of staff had been on annual leave and another on sick leave when the programme started. When they returned to work they were told about the new system but had a lot of other information to catch up on and did not pay full attention. When Mandy showed objects to the new members of staff, they were not sure what they were meant to do. On one occasion, they took her cup from her and put it in the dishwasher. As a result, Mandy found that pulling staff by the hand to where she wanted them was more effective than showing them objects because the objects only worked with some of the staff. The system soon collapsed as Mandy reverted to her old behaviour.

Get to know the person

Reading guidelines and talking to other staff is very important but nothing beats getting to know the people that use the service personally. As in any relationship, trust needs to be developed. Remember that each individual needs to get to know you as well and they might be just as anxious as you. A good way to build trust is to spend time with the person, doing activities that he or she enjoys.

Things that you need to find out about the people you are supporting include:

- how they communicate – the way they tell you what they want, what they like, what they do not want
- how they like to spend their time
- what they don't like doing
- what they like to eat and drink, and other preferences
- what they can do for themselves
- what they need support with
- their routines
- the order that they like to do things in

Keeping it Together © Pavilion Publishing (Brighton) Ltd 2007

- how long they take to do things
- their physical ability
- who they like.

Find out about the individual's history

While you are getting to know the person, you may want to read through some of their old notes. This will enable you get to know a little about their history. You can build a picture of how the person got to where they are today and some of the experiences they have had along the way. A word of caution, though! Everybody can change and our history does not necessarily mean that we are the same today (see **Box 2: Clive**).

Box 2: Clive

Clive is 50 years old. He lived with his mother until she died ten years ago. He then moved to a small supported house. This time was very distressing for Clive and he became quite withdrawn and was difficult to motivate.

One day at dinner, a member of staff was trying to get Clive to eat, because he had been off his food. Clive became angry and lashed out at the member of staff. Unfortunately, Clive still had his fork in his hand, and was labelled as trying to stab a member of staff.

Clive was transferred to a challenging behaviour service where the label of trying to stab a member of staff followed him. Since that incident, he had not presented any challenging behaviour. Unfortunately, however, the label stayed with him and it was very difficult to place him in a new home.

This example demonstrates how one incident can permanently change other people's perceptions of an individual.

Know the warning signs

If you know that someone's behaviour is likely to become challenging, it is a good idea to find out what the warning signs are. Although everybody is different, there are certain things that people do when they are becoming angry or irritated. These may well be a sign that the person's behaviour is about to become challenging. The following might be indicators to watch out for:

- faster or shallow breathing
- pacing up and down
- changes in speech – quieter, talking a lot faster or talking more than normal
- the person is staring more
- the person is puffing their chest out
- mumbling

- sweating
- being argumentative
- raising voice
- verbal threats or gestures
- swearing
- winding other people up
- the person can't keep their mind on what they are doing, when they normally can
- saying 'no' to something they would normally say 'yes' to
- erratic movements
- bodily tension and rigidity
- increased restlessness
- staring directly at you
- gritted teeth
- making their hands into fists
- asking lots of questions.

The guidelines should include indicators for each individual who uses the service. If they don't, you could ask the keyworker or someone who knows the people they support well, about how each person's behaviour changes if they are angry or irritated.

66 *It's okay to feel anxious, it's natural. I got to know the person and what made them tick. It was just like meeting anyone else. They get angry like anyone else, it's just more difficult finding out why.* 99

Quote from support worker

How to calm situations down and maintain safety

When you notice a person is starting to change and their behaviour might become challenging, you should try to do something as soon as possible before the situation becomes worse. Each person whose behaviour is known to become challenging should have reactive guidelines. Reactive guidelines give advice about what to do when the person's behaviour becomes a challenge. For someone whose behaviour has not been a challenge before, it might be a good idea to try the following.

Speaking and listening

- Talk clearly and slowly.
- Keep your voice at normal tone; do not shout or raise your voice.
- Listen carefully to what the person says.
- Give the person time.
- Ask them to tell you what has upset them.
- Acknowledge what the person says – you don't have to agree or disagree.
- If they are worried, reassure them.
- Do not blame the person for anything, and avoid blaming others.
- Do not make promises you cannot keep.
- Be non-judgemental and non-critical.
- Use non-threatening language.
- Appear calm, self-controlled and confident.
- Keep your body language calm and relaxed.
- Do not make threats.

Body language

The way we communicate is not just about what we say – we also communicate with our body language and facial expressions. The way we move can appear threatening or confrontational. You should:

- try to look relaxed
- don't fold your arms, point or wave your hands around
- try to keep your hands at your side
- stay at the same level as the person – if they are sitting, you should sit, and if they are standing, you should stand
- do not stand right in front of the person.

Eye contact

- Make eye contact.
- Try to make it look natural – most people glance away now and again when they are talking to someone.
- Do not try to stare the person down.

Space

- Do not invade the individual's personal space.
- Keep a safe distance between yourself and the person.
- Though the situation might not be at crisis point, you should keep the following at the back of your mind:
  - always know where your nearest exit is and keep yourself between the person whose behaviour is a challenge and the exit
  - do not back yourself into a corner.

Other people

- Make sure other staff are aware of the situation.
- Ensure your own and others' safety.
- Make sure you are not intimidating the person by surrounding them.
- Ask other staff members to support other people using the service.
- Remember that people are more important than the environment – for example, ensure your own safety before trying to save the television from damage.

Environment

- Look around you. Is there anything you could change that might stop the situation getting worse?
- Make sure the privacy, respect and dignity of the individual is upheld.
- Be aware of objects that might be used as weapons or could be thrown at you.

66 *If in doubt, do not deal with the situation alone. Call for assistance.* 99

Quote from a support worker

Things you can do if someone's behaviour becomes challenging

There are a number of things you can do when someone's behaviour becomes challenging. These are called reactive strategies. Reactive strategies should be agreed with your manager and staff. In certain circumstances (for example, when somebody's behaviour becomes challenging when their behaviour has not challenged you before), you will need to think on your feet. Some of the following techniques may be useful.

Redirection

Try redirecting the person into another activity, preferably a positive activity. This could include making something in the kitchen, going for a walk, playing a game or doing a household task. If you can get the person to take part in the activity, make sure you let them know how pleased you are (see *Box 3: Example of redirection*).

Box 3: Example of redirection

Neil is a man with severe learning disabilities and challenging behaviour who lives in a supported house. At times, Neil's behaviour can be challenging.

Mathew, a member of staff, had observed that whenever Neil starts becoming agitated, his breathing becomes faster and he starts repeating phrases to himself like, 'you shouldn't do that' or 'you mustn't punch him'.

Neil was in the lounge one day. His housemates were watching television but Neil wanted to change the channel. Mathew observed that Neil was breathing faster and starting to repeat his phrases.

Mathew immediately said to Neil, 'Shall we get your riding boots and hat, as you're going riding later this afternoon?' Neil enjoys horse riding, and getting his riding gear ready helped to distract him from what was happening in the lounge.

Relaxation

If the person is agitated, you could try helping them to calm down and relax. This could involve asking them to take deep breaths, listen to some calming music or spend some time alone. People can be taught to relax, and professionals such as a psychologist or occupational therapist might be able to help you to teach the people you support to relax (see *Box 4: Example of the use of relaxation*).

Box 4: Example of the use of relaxation

Sandy is a woman who can become agitated and then aggressive. However, there are usually some warning signs of when she is becoming agitated – her posture changes, she begins to sweat and she talks much faster than usual.

The occupational therapist has been working with Sandy for several weeks and has been teaching her to relax by a system of slowly relaxing each muscle in her body and by doing breathing exercises.

The staff can now observe when Sandy is becoming agitated by looking at her breathing and posture. They then encourage her to do her breathing exercises and remember the relaxed state the occupational therapist had shown her. This helps to prevent Sandy from becoming any more agitated and, with encouragement, she can be helped to relax again.

Remove the person or others from the situation

You could encourage the person to leave the situation, especially if it is something about the situation that is aggravating the person. If there are other people in the situation, you could ask them to leave (see *Box 5: Removing others from the situation*).

Box 5: Removing others from the situation

Claire is a woman who attends a day service for people with learning disabilities, which she enjoys. A bus comes to take Claire and some of the other people that use the service home at 3.30pm each day. The other people that use the service walk home, so stay on until 4pm. Some days, Claire will refuse to get on the bus. When Claire refuses to get on the bus, the staff team spend a long time trying to encourage Claire to get up – on one occasion, they even carried her out to the bus on the chair she was sitting on.

The staff team think that Claire might want to stay at the day service because she sees that the people who walk home stay there when she has to leave. They also feel that she enjoys having the attention of a lot of staff when they try to persuade her to get on the bus.

Because of this, the staff are trying something new. When Claire refuses to leave the day service, the staff ask everyone to leave the room Claire is in. The staff keep a minimum amount of contact, just enough to make sure she is okay.

After a few minutes of sitting alone, Claire gets up and leaves on her own. The staff give Claire lots of praise whenever she leaves on her own.

Change the environment

Think about the environment you are in; is there anything that you could change that might calm the situation down? Perhaps you could lower the noise levels or think about how hot or cold it is.

Maybe the person is bored and has not interacted with anyone for a long while. Is the person hungry, with no opportunity to get food because the kitchen is locked or because they need support to prepare food? Are the staff communicating with the person in a way that is hard for them to understand?

The things going on in the environment can be changed to suit the needs of each individual (see *Box 6: Example of change of environment*).

Box 6: Example of change of environment

Mark, a man with severe learning disabilities, was in the front room of his supported house. Mark had begun to punch himself repeatedly and Femi, a member of staff, went to try to calm him down.

When Femi got to the front room, she noticed the radio had been left on. The breakfast music show had finished and it was now tuned into a parliamentary debate programme. The television was also switched on, another person who lived there was in the room singing loudly to herself, the grandfather clock was chiming and the washing machine's spin cycle could be heard coming from the kitchen.

Femi walked around the room, switching off all the appliances, and closed the door. As the noise reduced, so did Mark's self-injury. There had probably been too much stimulation for Mark to take.

Talk to the person

This may seem obvious, but often we assume that people lack the skills to tell us why they are behaving in a particular way. Speech and language therapists are trained to help staff to understand how the person communicates.

Check the person is well

If someone suddenly starts displaying behaviour that you find challenging, it may be necessary to check whether they have a health problem. If someone has toothache, for example, it is likely to make them feel more irritable, not want to eat certain foods, and make them angry and short tempered, which staff could find challenging (see **Box 7: Sharon**).

Box 7: Sharon

Sharon had been aggressive to members of staff since she got out of bed. She had not eaten much of her breakfast and refused to go shopping, which she normally enjoys. After an hour of being up she refused to even stand up, and lay on the floor kicking out. A member of staff decided to remove her shoes, as her kicking could have hurt someone. When they took off Sharon's shoes, they discovered that she had a drawing pin in her foot, which had been the cause of her behaviour that morning.

If you give someone PRN (meaning 'when needed') medication such as paracetamol in the event of a health problem, and the person's challenging behaviour decreases after you have given them the painkillers, it could indicate that their behaviour was due to a physical health problem. *Note: any medication given to someone that you support should be prescribed by his or her doctor.*

In circumstances where there may be a health problem, a visit to the GP may be advisable so that the person can have a health check. This is not something that you can do immediately if someone's behaviour is challenging, but it should be done as soon as it is safe to do so.

Use of restraint

Restraint means holding someone so they cannot move. This includes restraining them by locking them in a room or strapping them to a wheelchair. Most services don't agree with the use of restraint. In some circumstances, very specialist services have staff who are trained to use restraint. If restraint is used, the following guidelines need to be followed:

- Restraint should always be the last resort after all other methods have failed.
- Restraint should only be used as part of a complete care package, where other ways of working with the person are included too.
- The staff using restraint need to have specialist training before they attempt to use it.
- Training needs to be ongoing, with regular updates.
- Training in restraint should be accompanied by training on how to work with people whose behaviour is challenging without the need for restraint (for example, by using defusing techniques).
- Policies and procedures need to be in place (for example, debriefing or de-escalation).
- The correct number of staff needs to be on duty to undertake restraint safely.
- Staff working in a service that uses restraint need to be regularly supervised.
- Members of the multi-disciplinary team need to be involved in designing the restraint policy.
- Incidents where restraint is used need to be recorded and reviewed.
- Restraint should be used for the shortest time possible.

Reasons why it is best not to use restraint

It is always better if we do not use restraint. Some of the reasons for this are:

- Having to restrain someone is degrading for the person being restrained.
- Restraint could cause injuries to the person you are trying to support and members of staff.
- Restraint could be used inappropriately – for example, it could be seen as a method of punishing someone.

- Having to restrain someone could cause personal conflicts in your role as a support worker (i.e. you might be supporting someone one day and having to restrain them the next day). This could damage the relationship you have built up with the person.

- Restraining someone does not solve the problems that lead to the challenging behaviour in the first place.

Where you work, you need to use the policies that are given to you. Some staff may have adopted methods that you are concerned about. You might feel that some members of staff are acting in a way that you feel is abusive. If you have any concerns, you should always raise them with your manager.

For further information on restraint, read the British Institute of Learning Disabilities Code of Practice for the use of Physical Interventions (see ***Appendix Two: Bibliography and resources***).

Conclusion

When faced with challenging behaviour, we are likely to feel scared, especially the first few times it happens. This is perfectly normal. There are many ways to spot that someone's behaviour may be becoming challenging and much can be done to help to defuse a situation.

section two

Understanding challenging behaviour

This section looks at the different types of challenging behaviour, the impact that challenging behaviour has, why it happens, how it has been dealt with in the past and how we try to support people whose behaviour we find a challenge today.

The term 'challenging behaviour' is often used in services for people with learning disabilities. But it can mean different things to different people. What one person finds challenging, another person might find acceptable. For example, a parent of two young children might have a high tolerance for noise levels, whereas someone who lives alone might find the same noise levels very challenging. In the same way, some services may be accustomed to challenging behaviour, and others may have never experienced challenging behaviour or may have differing ideas about what they think it is.

Challenging behaviour refers to:

' *Behaviours that have a negative impact on the person's quality of life or the quality of life of the people with whom they live.'*

Baker, 2002

Types of challenging behaviour

The main types of challenging behaviour are shown in **Box 8: The main types of challenging behaviour.**

Box 8: The main types of challenging behaviour	
Self-injurious behaviour	*Aggression towards others*
This is where people hurt themselves. It includes punching, scratching, biting or pinching themselves, and hitting themselves against objects – for example, banging their head against the wall.	This is where the person is verbally or physically aggressive to other people. It includes shouting, calling people offensive names, punching, kicking, scratching or biting.
Anti-social behaviour	*Destruction of property*
This includes screaming, spitting, smearing faeces, or taking clothes off in inappropriate places.	This includes damage to property such as smashing furniture, breaking windows or ripping clothes.

Why call it challenging behaviour?

In the past, this type of behaviour has been called disruptive, problem or bad behaviour. The person was commonly seen as being the problem. We no longer see the person as the problem; instead, it is a challenge for us to find out why the person is behaving in this way and to provide them with appropriate support. It is not the person that is challenging, but their behaviour. It is we that need to change, to provide more effective support to the individual.

How does challenging behaviour impact on someone's quality of life and on the lives of others?

Challenging behaviour can result in unwanted things happening for all those involved (see the examples in **Box 9: Jack**, **Box 10: Sukie's story** and **Box 11: Tim's story**).

Consequences for the person whose behaviour is challenging

- They may be rejected by those around them.
- They might not be able to get out of the house as much.
- They may be physically harmed.
- They may have fewer opportunities, inside and outside the house.
- They may experience aggression from other people using the service.
- People (including staff) may react to the person in an unacceptable or abusive way.
- The person may be made to live in a specialist house, where they may have fewer opportunities to do things.

Box 9: Jack

Jack shares his home with three other people with learning disabilities. Staff support is provided 24 hours a day. Jack moved here from his parents' home a few months ago. He cannot speak and does not use any sign language. Recently, Jack has not been himself. He sometimes hits the staff and other people he lives with. His also screams very loudly when the staff do not understand his needs.

Jack tends to spend a lot of time by himself nowadays. The staff help him with his basic needs like washing and dressing, but tend to leave him alone at other times. The people Jack lives with avoid him; sometimes they leave the room when he walks in and refuse to go out of the house with him.

Consequences for the other people using the service

- They may be hurt by the person whose behaviour is challenging.
- They might have feelings of rejection.
- They can feel unsafe.
- They might isolate themselves by, for example, staying in their bedroom.
- They may start to have behaviour that challenges as well.
- Staff may spend a lot of time supporting the person whose behaviour is challenging, and have less time for other people they support as a result.

Box 10: Sukie's story

Sukie lives in the same house as Jack. She is a friendly person, who enjoys the company of others. Since Jack moved in, the staff have seen a change in Sukie. She tends to spend a lot more time in her bedroom now. She will only come out if Jack is not around or if staff are with her. When she is in the company of others, she is much quieter than normal, especially if Jack is in the room. She tries to avoid him as much as possible. Jack has hit Sukie several times and on one occasion gave her a black eye.

Consequences for staff

- You may be hurt by the person whose behaviour is challenging.
- You may feel the person doesn't like you.
- You may feel that you do not know what to do.
- Your work might make you feel stressed out.
- You may have increased sickness and more time off work.
- You may feel that it is your fault.
- You may feel scared.

Box 11: Tim's story

Tim is Jack's keyworker. He has worked in the house for five years and has developed good relationships with the people who live there and the staff. When Jack moved in, Tim was appointed as his keyworker. Tim has tried to get to know Jack. He has set up a timetable of activities, but Jack rarely appears to join in. Jack tends to hit out at staff when they try to engage him in activities, and one staff member received several bruises on her body. Since then, the staff have been reluctant to engage Jack. Most of them are frightened of him. Staff sickness tends to increase when staff know they are on the rota to take Jack out shopping.

Tim doesn't know what to do. He thinks he should be able to solve the situation as he is Jack's keyworker, but cannot think of a solution. He has tried his best but nothing seems to work.

Why does challenging behaviour happen?

Challenging behaviour does not occur without a reason, although finding that reason can be very difficult and frustrating. People with learning disabilities may use behaviour that we find challenging in order to cope with what is going on around them.

For example, if we are bored one weekend, we can find a variety of things to do. We might phone friends, look through the cinema listings, invite people for dinner, go to a sporting event or throw a party. Someone with learning disabilities who is bored on a weekend may have to rely on staff for support. See the example of Samuel opposite.

> Samuel has a severe learning disability and no verbal communication.

▼

> He is bored, sitting in the front room of his home.

▼

> He does not have any activities to do – one member of staff is cleaning, the other is doing paperwork.

▼

> He does not know how to ask the staff to support him in an activity.

▼

> He knows that, if he bangs his hand on the window for long enough, a member of staff will come.

▼

> He starts to bang the window. After a minute, one of the staff tells him to stop banging.

When we look at what is happening to Samuel, we can see that he is banging the window because he is bored and needs something to do. When he bangs the window, he gets to interact with a member of staff for a few seconds when they enter the room to tell him off. The member of staff may view Samuel as being 'mad', 'a pain in the neck', 'a trouble-maker', 'someone who is nasty' or 'someone on a wind-up'. The member of staff may feel this way because they are busy trying to get their work done and Samuel is interrupting them.

Because challenging behaviour has a reason, it is very important that we do not see it as being 'part of the person'. Once we start seeing the person as the problem, or believe they are deliberately trying to annoy us, we are less likely to want to help them.

In Samuel's case, the member of staff doing the cleaning could have asked Samuel to help and the problem may have been solved. The member of staff would have got their job done and Samuel would have got to do the activity. Samuel could be stopped from banging the windows by changing what is going on around him. When we are really upset by a person's behaviour, we might think they need to be restrained or given tablets, or that they should be moved to another house. But what we really need to do is change the way we work with the person.

What happened in the past?

In the past, people with learning disabilities either lived with their families or in large institutions. Families were encouraged to place family members who had learning disabilities into institutions, especially if their behaviour was challenging.

These institutions were usually on the outskirts of towns and cities, where the 'patients' were considered to be protected from society and society was safe from them.

How did we deal with challenging behaviour?

Many of the methods that were once used by the institutions to deal with challenging behaviour are now considered to be unethical.

The institutions used punishment and seclusion as ways of controlling the people who lived in them.

When psychiatric drugs were introduced, many people with learning disabilities were given medication in the hope that this might control their behaviour, even if they did not have a mental health problem.

Ways of changing behaviour by giving rewards or by punishment were adapted to deal with unwanted behaviours in people with learning disabilities. These could be effective in reducing unwanted behaviour, but they did not help individuals to learn new, appropriate ways of behaving. The unwanted behaviour may have been reduced by these methods, but it could also be replaced by other unwanted behaviours (see the example in *Box 12: Lesley*).

Box 12: Lesley

Lesley, a woman with severe learning disabilities, lives in a supported home. Lesley used to scream for long periods of time. The staff working with her found this distressing and would often put on her favourite CDs and dance with her to stop her from screaming. At a staff meeting, the staff team decided that Lesley's screaming was 'attention seeking' and they agreed that when Lesley screamed in future they would ignore the screaming, no matter how bad it got.

Lesley's screaming got worse over the next week but the staff remained resolute and ignored the screams. Eventually, Lesley stopped screaming. But unfortunately, she also began to strip off her clothes in the living room. The staff would have to run to cover Lesley up and a great fuss would be made as she and the other people living with her were moved so she could be dressed. Lesley's previous challenging behaviour had been replaced with a new behaviour that was even more difficult to deal with.

Why punishment does not work

The reason punishment will not work in the long term is because we are just removing a behaviour we do not like, not its cause. So, in the example in *Box 12: Lesley*, Lesley's screaming was simply replaced by her taking her clothes off instead.

Also, for punishment to work, the person needs to understand that the punishment (which may take place well after the behaviour) is linked to a particular previous behaviour.

In addition to this, it is very likely that an adult whose behaviour is challenging has been punished since their childhood, and yet still has behaviours that we find a challenge. This demonstrates that in the long term, punishment is not effective.

Punishment is also unethical.

What is our approach nowadays?

Today, approaches to challenging behaviour have changed. We no longer punish people to try to reduce behaviours we do not like. Using punishment may reduce unwanted behaviour, but it can be seen as unethical (see *Box 13: Mark*).

Box 13: Mark

Mark has a severe learning disability and autism, is non-verbal and lives in a large hospital for people with learning disabilities.

Mark will self-injure by punching himself in the side of the head, which causes a great deal of distress to the staff team working with him. The staff team asked for help and were told to put Mark's arms in splints so that he could no longer injure himself. Whenever Mark's arms were put into splints, however, he would bang his head against a wall and sustain far greater damage, so the splints were withdrawn.

A new idea has been suggested that, whenever Mark self-injures, a foul-tasting substance is squirted into his mouth. It is hoped that he will stop self-injuring when he begins to associate the punishing taste with punching himself. Lemon juice, chilli sauce and shaving cream have all been suggested as ways of punishing Mark.

Ethical issues

- It is socially unacceptable.
- You should not inflict pain on someone.
- Mark has not consented, and nor has he been given a choice.
- No assessment has been carried out to find out why Mark may be hitting himself (i.e. the function of his behaviour).
- There has been no physical health check to look for something like earache or toothache, which may be reasons why he is hitting himself.
- If using arm splints made a new challenging behaviour develop, this probably will too.

Today, interventions look at building on an individual's existing strengths or teaching new, appropriate behaviour, rather than just trying to get rid of unwanted behaviours (see ***Box 14: Lesley – a modern approach***). If someone has new skills, they are less likely to use behaviours we find a challenge.

Box 14: Lesley — a modern approach

Earlier (in **Box 12: Lesley**), we discussed how staff ignored Lesley's screaming to try to stop the behaviour.

Today, we would still not want Lesley to scream but we would try to find ways that would make Lesley not need to scream.

In Lesley's case, it was found that:

- Lesley was often left for long periods of time with nothing to do
- Lesley had never been taught to operate the CD player on her own, so was reliant on staff
- staff could not spend time with Lesley as they had to do the cleaning and prepare dinner.

What the staff team did to help with this behaviour

- In the past, when the staff were cleaning or preparing dinner, Lesley was left alone in the lounge. Now, they supported Lesley to clean her house and prepare her own meals, instead of doing it for her. This meant Lesley was occupied in meaningful activity, she learned new skills and had a wider range of activities other than just listening to music. She was also guaranteed staff attention while she was cleaning and cooking.

- Staff taught Lesley to use the CD player, by putting a large blue sticker on the open/close button and a large red sticker on the play button. Lesley was then able to operate the CD player independently.

- Staff assigned time to listen to Lesley's music, and dance with her each day. Lesley began to realise that this would happen every day. She began to adapt to her new routine and to realise what would happen next.

An occupational therapist and a speech and language therapist helped the team to develop these ideas.

Conclusion

Challenging behaviour often arises due to an individual's environment not being suitable for their needs. The environment could mean where they live, the day service they attend or the staff who are working with them. We no longer look at trying to get rid of the behaviour. We now look at changing what is going on around the people we support, so that they do not need to use behaviours that we find a challenge.

section three

What to do next

This section covers communicating with others following an incident of challenging behaviour. Communication can be verbal or written. This section will give you some examples of how to achieve effective communication.

Telling others about what happened

Whenever there is an incident of challenging behaviour, it is important that you write down what happened. This information may help you to identify triggers, draw up future guidelines and help other members of staff.

It is important that you try to record what has happened as soon as possible after the incident, because the information will still be fresh in your mind. You may be tempted to write why you think events have happened but it is best simply to write about what you saw and know to have occurred. You should write what happened before and after the event, and include when, what and where.

You may be asked to keep special records, such as ABC charts, incident forms or daily diaries; your service will have policies on these. An ABC chart is for writing down what happened before, during and after challenging behaviour. (For information on completing ABC charts, see **Section Five: Working in the long term**.)

Talk to the manager/keyworker

You should inform your manager of any behaviours that you have found challenging, as there may be a potential future risk. Reporting an incident is not an admission that you have failed or that you are not good enough. Managers have a duty of care to their staff to see that they are not put at risk. Your manager and other members of staff may be able to talk through any emotions or problems that you are having at work. Supervision is a good way for you to raise any concerns that you have (supervision is covered in **Section Four: Helping yourselves**).

Handover

You need to explain any difficulties that you have experienced during your shift to the people starting the next shift. If someone has been agitated that morning and you do not pass this information on, the afternoon staff could be at risk. This is especially so if they are planning activities, perhaps in the community away from other staff support.

If you have a format for handover where you can discuss each of the people that use the service or talk through a written report, this will make sure that no details are missed. Your manager should make sure that there is enough time for staff to discuss issues at handover.

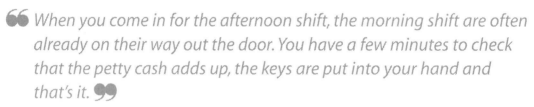

When you come in for the afternoon shift, the morning shift are often already on their way out the door. You have a few minutes to check that the petty cash adds up, the keys are put into your hand and that's it.

Support worker discussing a poor handover

Communication book

A communication book can allow you to provide information to the whole staff team, even when you are not going to come into direct contact with them. Messages may not get passed on by word of mouth, especially if someone is on a day off or annual leave.

Team meetings

Team meetings are a good opportunity to gather information from the whole team and get everyone's thoughts. Incidents that have happened can also be discussed.

Team meetings can be a good platform for staff to talk about their concerns. Unfortunately, these meetings may be more concerned with the everyday running of the service, and time may be taken up talking about shopping and budgets before the people that use the service are discussed.

If there is limited time for team meetings, issues concerning the people that use the service should be placed at the top of the agenda.

It is essential that you write down what was said in team meetings, so that everyone who was there can remember it, and for the benefit of those who did not attend. Any decisions from the meeting also need to be followed up.

Conclusion

When we are faced with challenging behaviour, we need to report it immediately. By reporting incidents, you are not admitting that you failed or that you have done anything wrong. Reporting incidents helps to plan for the future and maintain safety. This needs to be done both verbally, by telling someone, and in writing.

section four

Helping yourselves

This section covers how you can support yourself as an individual, how you can support yourself within your organisation and how you can support yourself to work more effectively with the people that use your service.

Helping yourselves as individuals

Coping with stress

What is stress?

Stress can be described as unpleasant feelings or sensations experienced when excessive demands are placed on us. This could happen in our home life (when we have demands from our family) or in our work life (when the pressures of the job exceed our ability to cope with them).

Stress at work

Stress at work is unavoidable and in some cases it can be good. For example, stress is what makes us meet deadlines or get through difficult or tricky situations. However, only the right amount of stress is beneficial. Too much stress can have a detrimental effect on the individual.

It is in a service's best interests to look at the levels of stress their staff are under, because too much stress can lead to:

- poor timekeeping
- poor work output
- conflict between members of staff
- loss of motivation
- increased sickness or absence.

Eventually, stress at work could lead to illness, which can be viewed as an industrial injury and should be taken seriously.

How you might feel when you are stressed

Physical symptoms

- Muscular tension
- Aches
- Pains
- Headaches
- Difficulty sleeping
- Nausea
- Feeling light-headed
- Chest pains
- Loss of appetite
- Diarrhoea or constipation
- Pains in stomach
- Conditions like asthma or eczema may get worse
- Shallow breathing
- Problems eating or swallowing
- Dry mouth
- Lump in the throat
- Unable to concentrate
- Tired
- Shaky hands
- Racing or pounding heart
- Pins and needles
- Feeling faint

Psychological/emotional/behavioural symptoms

- Tearfulness/depression
- Anxiety
- Poor decision-making skills
- Loss of creativity
- Moodiness
- Loss of libido (sex drive)
- Anger
- Loss of motivation
- Lack of concentration
- Loss of sense of humour
- Relationship problems
- Irritation
- Frustration
- Wanting to smoke or drink alcohol more than usual

The feelings we get when we are under stress date back to our basic survival instincts. When we are faced with danger, our brain makes sure our body is pumped full of hormones to help us either run away or deal with the danger. This is often called the 'fight or flight' response.

We still have this response to danger today, and it can be very helpful if someone tries to rob you in the street on a dark night. In modern society, we have new dangers such as the fear of getting the sack, finding childcare or making mortgage repayments, and these can all put us under stress.

Most of us have felt the effects of stress at some point in our lives, perhaps when we have had to sit exams, go for a job interview or take a driving test. We may have felt some of the symptoms listed earlier. Usually, we return to normal after the exam or test and the symptoms fade away. Problems occur when the stress continues for long periods of time, which can be associated with health problems.

How to reduce your stress levels

Relaxation training

It is impossible for your body to be relaxed and in a state of high anxiety at the same time. Relaxation therefore helps combat stress, as it is the opposite sensation. Relaxation helps to switch off the hormones that are associated with stress. Some of us may need to be taught how to relax and become aware of how our bodies feel when they are tense. There are various methods that can be used, which are listed in *Box 15: Relaxation techniques*.

Keep a stress diary

Being able to anticipate when stress may occur makes it easier to deal with. Diaries can help understand the causes of short-term stress in your life. By keeping a diary of your mood and stress levels at particular times of the day and particular days of the week, you can examine whether you are worse in the morning or afternoon, or feel more stressed when you have particular meetings, have to speak in front of others or supporting a specific individual or staff member. You should record when you are not at work as well, to see whether you have stressors in your home life, and find out what helps you to calm down outside work.

Exercise

Exercise can be helpful in combating stress, because it releases bodily chemicals called endorphins, which help you to relax naturally. Exercise gives you the opportunity to clear your mind and helps regulate your breathing, and stretching before and after exercise can release muscle tension. Exercise can also improve your sleep patterns, which can be disrupted if you are under stress.

Relaxing activities

Making sure that you spend some time in activities that relax you can be important. Taking even a few minutes a day to do what you enjoy, such as listening to music or watching a favourite television programme or film can help. Activities like massage can help by reducing muscle tension and helping you to relax.

Diet

Our diet can have a profound affect on the way we feel and think. Stimulants like coffee can crank up how alert we feel, which can be detrimental to someone who is already stressed. Caffeine can also disrupt sleep patterns by keeping us up at night, which can have a negative effect on efforts to combat stress.

Alcohol is often used as a route to relaxation and will temporarily eliminate any stresses we may have been under. However, whatever has been causing us stress will probably still be there the next day and we will now have to deal with it with the addition of a hangover. Alcohol, when taken in large quantities, also disrupts the body's hormones, blood sugar levels and brain chemicals. As with recreational drugs, it needs to be remembered that what goes up must come down.

It is important to make sure that we eat a healthy diet. When we are under stress, we may not eat properly or may seek comfort foods. A well balanced diet will help to regulate ordinary bodily functions that can be disrupted by stress.

Share your problems

You should share any problems that you are having at work with your manager, or at least discuss them among your peers. Your manager may be able to find ways of helping you within the workplace. By discussing problems with workmates, you may find you are not alone or they may be able to tell you ways they have dealt with the same problems themselves.

Outside the work setting, sharing problems with friends or family can help to relieve some of the pressures or burdens that you have been carrying alone. Friends and family may be able to relieve you of some of the pressures that you may be under out of work, reducing stress in other areas of your life.

You will need to remember that you are bound by confidentiality if you are discussing specific issues at work.

Keeping it Together © Pavilion Publishing (Brighton) Ltd 2007

Box 15: Relaxation techniques

Progressive muscle relaxation

This is a systematic approach to relaxation, where someone is taught how to physically relax their muscles. The programme involves tensing then resting individual muscles one by one, so the person becomes aware of what being relaxed feels like. There are audiocassettes and CDs available that can help to teach someone progressive muscle relaxation.

Guided relaxation

This involves imagining relaxing scenarios. The participant first makes himself or herself comfortable and takes a relaxed position. They are then encouraged to remember a moment in their life when they felt they were relaxed or happy. Common themes are relaxing on a beach or indulging in a favourite relaxing pastime. Any scenario that is relaxing can be used, as long as it does not trigger other sad or stressful memories.

Meditation

Meditation has been used by most major religions for many thousands of years. Devotees to religious meditation may be required to undertake specific rituals. However, meditation can be achieved without subscribing to any particular religious ideas. Meditation involves clearing the mind of all thoughts, which is often not easy when you have stressful events regularly jumping into your mind. It can help to focus on an object like a flower or a candle, or repeat a phrase over and over to yourself.

Breathing exercises

Breathing exercises can help us to relax because they give us something to focus on, and prevent the rapid breathing that is often associated with stress. Breathing exercises can help us to maintain the correct levels of oxygen in our body, which can increase when we breathe too rapidly.

Yoga/T'ai Chi

These are disciplines that come from ancient India and China. They involve physical exercises, co-ordinated movements and ways to regulate breathing that have been found to relax the body and mind.

Helping yourselves organisationally

There is a variety of ways in which you can help yourselves as an organisation when faced with challenging behaviour. The way you organise each shift, the activities that you provide, and how you communicate with each other and the people you support can all be used to help. This section demonstrates how we can support people whose behaviour is challenging.

Risk assessment/management

Risk assessments are necessary when someone's behaviour is challenging. Often, staff feel intimidated about drawing up a risk assessment but the process need not be that complicated.

Basically, risk assessment looks at all the things that might go wrong when we are managing a situation or trying something new. If we can find out what problems might arise and why, we can do something about them.

Risk management aims to reduce the likelihood that harm will happen. Once you have tried to minimise harm, a contingency plan needs to be put into place. Contingency plans are a 'safety net' in case something goes wrong. We will cover these later.

Box 16: Colin gives an example of how challenging behaviour can impact on a person's independence, inclusion, choice and respect. In Colin's case, the staff are worried about taking him out.

Box 16: Colin

Colin is a 25-year-old man who has a severe learning disability and autism. He can use some words to communicate his basic needs, such as 'drink', 'eat' and 'toilet'. It is extremely rare for Colin to initiate conversation.

At times, Colin can become agitated and will start to say 'bad boy' repeatedly. Staff have found that sometimes, after a few minutes of saying 'bad boy', Colin will become physically aggressive. The challenging needs team has been supporting the staff team in assessing Colin's behaviour. The team has found that he is more likely to become aggressive in noisy environments, when he is asked to do something he does not want to do, and when staff do not respond immediately after he has requested a drink.

Colin's interests include listening to his personal stereo and spending time in the garden. He also loves buses, especially double-deckers. When walking in the street, he becomes very excited whenever he sees a bus go by.

Colin's keyworker has suggested that he could have a weekly trip on a bus. Some of the team are not so keen on this idea. They are worried about Colin's aggression and feel they might not be able to cope if he became aggressive on a bus. They are also worried that they might not be able to get him off the bus.

Risk assessment for Colin

There are several benefits to Colin being supported to travel by bus but, unfortunately, there are also a number of things that may go wrong, and these may impact on Colin. For example, Colin may refuse to get off the bus and he may become physically aggressive to staff or others on the bus.

Keeping it Together © Pavilion Publishing (Brighton) Ltd 2007

As a result of aggressive behaviour:

- Colin may get banned from using the local buses, which could lead to him being socially excluded again
- Colin may cause embarrassment to himself and others
- Colin's physical aggression could lead to the police being called
- a member of the public who does not understand the situation may assault Colin, or the staff member with him.

When we see the list of things that can go wrong and the consequences of taking the risk, we might immediately think that the risk is not worth taking.

What we also need to do, therefore, is list the positives that may come out of taking this risk. For example:

- Colin will be involved in an activity he will probably enjoy, and this should improve his quality of life
- it will broaden his participation in community activities
- he will learn new skills such as handling money, waiting and crossing the road, which can be transferred to other areas of his life
- it will increase his social contacts and networks
- he will learn from positive role models
- it will increase his independence
- he will widen his experiences.

When we balance up the positives that Colin might gain, it makes us realise that Colin should be supported to take this risk. However, the risk needs to be managed in the right way. From the information we have been given, we can come up with some ideas about how we can minimise potential dangers. Some ideas are listed below.

- Colin doesn't like noise or crowds, so a time of day could be chosen when the buses are less busy, so they are emptier and quieter.

- Colin likes to wear his personal stereo so if he takes this with him it might help provide a distraction if it is noisy.

- One of the staff concerns is that Colin may not get off the bus. If the final destination is somewhere Colin can do an activity he likes, it may make it more likely that Colin will get off. For example, Colin likes to be in the garden so a journey to gardens or a park may be motivating for him.

- If the bus terminates at the bus garage and everyone else gets off, this might be a clear signal to Colin that it is time to get off the bus.

- Colin could begin by travelling on the bus for only a few stops, so he gets used to travelling on buses before attempting longer distances.

- Two members of staff could accompany Colin initially, until he is settled into the new activity. The number of staff can then be reduced.

- Taking a flask with him should get rid of the problem of not meeting Colin's request for a drink.

- Saying 'bad boy' repeatedly is a warning, so staff know that if Colin is saying 'bad boy', a problem could be imminent. If Colin starts saying 'bad boy' they could decide to turn around and come home at that point, rather than waiting until it develops into a more severe problem. If Colin starts saying 'bad boy' before the excursion, it could be postponed until he is ready to go out.

Even when we have put all our ideas in place, we can't guarantee that Colin won't become aggressive. Nor can we plan for the unexpected, such as the bus breaking down, bad weather or an unexpectedly busy journey. In these eventualities we need to put **contingency plans** in place. Contingency plans will not stop the worst from happening, but they do help when something does go wrong.

Examples of contingency plans are:

- carrying a mobile phone so that you can call for assistance or advice

- taking taxi numbers and cab fare with you so that you have an alternative route home

- having an ID badge or information card that can be used to explain (while respecting confidentiality), if there is a problem.

It can be seen that risk management is not that complex. First, we look at what could possibly go wrong, by examining the history of the individual we are supporting and the environment around them. We then try to come up with as many ideas as possible that could reduce the likelihood that these problems will happen. This is done by trying to make changes in the environment – for example, in Colin's case, by taking a drink with him on the bus. We can also reduce problems by using Colin's strengths, like his interest in the garden leading us to choose a garden as a possible destination.

Shift planning

Like any household, residential services need to be organised. However, in a supported home, planning needs to be even more precise. Diaries and shift planners can help with this, and can help provide the people we support with meaningful activities both inside and outside the house.

Most of us plan in advance and organise our lives so that we know when we are on shift and when we have training, annual leave, doctor's appointments or days off. Most people keep track by writing appointments in a diary or on a calendar. In a busy learning disability service used by a number of people, and with up to three shift changes a day, keeping track of what is going on and who does what is even more complicated. In these circumstances, a diary alone may not be enough.

For example:

- some members of staff may be assigned to support more than one person
- agency staff who are new to the house may not know routines, and may need direction
- activities might be forgotten if they are not written down.

In such cases, more structured methods of planning will probably be needed.

Most services have a weekly timetable for each of the people using the service, stating the activities they might have on each day of the week. These can be helpful, but a more detailed method of day-to-day planning can be used by breaking the day into hours (see **Box 17: Plan for Monday morning shift in a small group home**, which shows how a basic shift plan might look).

Box 17: Plan for Monday morning shift in a small group home

Day: Monday a.m. shift   **Staff on duty:** Monette and David

Time	Simon	Support worker	Mel	Support worker	Marcus	Support worker
08.00	Get up (wash and dress independently)		Get up, supported to wash and dress	Monette	Get up (wash and dress independently — supported to shave)	David
09.00	Supported to prepare breakfast	David	Supported to prepare breakfast	Monette		
10.00	Write shopping list	Monette	Load dishwasher		Supported to prepare breakfast	David
11.00	Put laundry on		Hoover lounge with support	Monette	Unload dishwasher	David
12.00	Transfer washing to dryer, pack bag and make sandwiches for college		Go to bank, shopping and video library	Monette	Water the garden	David
13.00	Catch bus to college		Supported to prepare and eat lunch	Monette	Dentist	David
14.00			Put dishes in dishwasher	Monette	Supported to prepare and eat lunch	David

This plan shows exactly what the two support staff, Monette and David, are doing at each time of the day, and whom they should be supporting. Shift plans can be much more detailed than this and will vary depending on the type of service and the number of people that use it. If you would like further information about planning shifts, please see the *Active Support* handbook (Jones *et al*, 1997), which describes in far greater detail how to do this.

We also need to consider the different times of year, as activities will change between summer and winter. People who attend sessions that are dependent on the season need to have alternative support in place when their normal activities are not available.

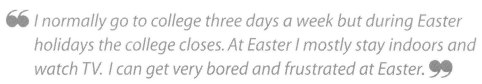

I normally go to college three days a week but during Easter holidays the college closes. At Easter I mostly stay indoors and watch TV. I can get very bored and frustrated at Easter.

Man with a learning disability talking about college

Supervision

Supervision is a two-way process, where junior staff can discuss work-related issues with a senior member of staff (usually their line manager) who has more experience. The supervisor's role is to support and guide the supervisee through problems they might encounter, within a relationship that is based on trust. Supervision should not be a managerial process of delegating jobs or checking up on people. Junior staff should be made to feel comfortable about talking about their problems.

Communication within the team

Communication within a team will either be verbal or written.

Verbal communication includes things such as the handover between outgoing and incoming shifts, or discussions in meetings.

Written communication involves the notes that are recorded during or at the end of a shift, minutes from meetings, care plans and guidelines or ABC charts.

Communication within the organisation

Your organisation will have its own routes of communication. For instance, incident forms will need to be completed whenever there has been a serious incident, such as someone being harmed. Accident forms may need to be completed too.

Keeping it Together © Pavilion Publishing (Brighton) Ltd 2007

On-call systems

On-call systems involve staff being able to contact a senior member of staff when there are emergencies or issues that they do not feel confident with. On-call systems usually work during out-of-office hours or when there is minimal staffing, such as during a night shift.

When a member of staff finds that someone they are supporting has behaviour they find a challenge, they should be able to contact a senior member of staff for assistance.

Training

Training can help to improve the knowledge, skills and attitudes of staff. In the absence of appropriate guidance, we are left to make our own decisions about what we should do. Staff should be given time off to attend training on challenging behaviour, as well as mandatory training such as food hygiene.

Helping yourselves better support people whose behaviour is challenging

By examining the way you provide activities and the type of support that is on offer, you can identify a number of things that can help you to support a person better.

Engaging the people you support in activities

You need to be aware of the way the person communicates or how much they understand of what you are saying (see *Box 18: Offering people activities* for an example).

Box 18: Offering people activities

Angela is a woman with autism, who lives in a supported house. Angela is passionate about soap operas and likes to watch her favourite soaps in the evening. The staff are trying to encourage the people living there to become involved in the way their house is run. Whenever Angela is asked if she will do the washing up after dinner, however, she becomes very agitated and starts swearing. The staff have checked that this activity does not clash with any of her favourite television programmes, so they cannot understand why it gets her so upset.

The occupational therapist suggests this could be due to Angela's autism, which is associated with problems around imagination. The occupational therapist explains that Angela might have a problem imagining when the task will end and may think that if the task goes on too long it will clash with her soap operas.

That evening, the staff suggest that Angela wash up four plates and then she can move on to another activity. The staff find that Angela is happy to do this, as she understands exactly what is expected. The staff realise that it was the way they offered activities that caused problems, rather than the activities themselves.

The level of support that you offer

Different people require different levels of support. Some may just need to be told what the task is, whereas others may need a more 'hands-on' approach. For example, someone with a more severe learning disability may need to be shown how to carry out a task, or may even need to be guided by the member of support staff holding their hands to demonstrate.

An individual you are supporting may need only to be asked to carry out some parts of a task, but may require a greater level of support to carry out more difficult parts. For example, getting ingredients out of the fridge is easier than weighing them and mixing them to make a cake. So supporting someone to make a cake may require the support worker to vary the level of support they give throughout the task.

Knowing how the individuals you support communicate

Not all people with learning disabilities communicate in the same way. We cannot presume that what we are trying to say is being understood the way we intend. A complex conversation that has a number of instructions may be difficult for someone with learning disabilities to follow. A sentence such as 'Could you get the cup that's on the table and put it into the bowl in the sink?' includes a number of different instructions. First, the cup has to be picked up. Second, the cup is on the table. Third, it has to be put into the bowl. Fourth, the bowl is in the sink. An intricate sentence with so many instructions might be too complex for someone with a learning disability (see ***Box 19: Too many instructions***).

Box 19: Too many instructions

Sarah attends a day service for people with learning disabilities. Staff have found Sarah's behaviour at lunch increasingly challenging. Sarah will sometimes throw her cup across the dining room, and staff are worried that one day it might hit someone.

In desperation, the staff start to threaten Sarah with, 'If you throw that cup one more time, you won't get dessert'. Whenever Sarah hears this threat, it seems to encourage her to throw her cup even more. As a consequence, Sarah has not had dessert all week and has become even more agitated as a result.

A speech and language therapist who is carrying out an assessment of Sarah tells the staff team that Sarah understands only a limited number of keywords in a sentence, and that she does not understand negative words like 'shouldn't', 'won't', 'can't' and 'hasn't'. The speech and language therapist believes that when Sarah hears 'If you throw that cup one more time, you won't get dessert,' she probably only understands 'throw – cup – dessert'. So the increase in cup throwing could actually be a result of the staff threats – Sarah may be throwing the cup because she thinks she will get dessert if she throws it, not that she won't.

Note: As we discussed earlier, it is unethical to punish someone in this way, whether the person understands the instruction or not.

Tips to assist with communication

- Keep sentences short.
- Only use one concept per sentence.
- Avoid specialist or technical jargon.
- Use short, everyday words.
- Avoid abstract words if possible (abstract concepts are things that we cannot see, like our feelings or the future).
- Use positives, not negatives. For example:
  - 'If you **don't** put your shoes on, we **won't** be able to go outside' (negative)
  - 'Put your shoes on so that we can go outside' (positive).
- Ask a speech and language therapist for advice.

Making things predictable – timetables, routines, structure

We all like things to be predictable. We have diaries, wear watches and keep calendars so that we can plan for events in the future and know what is about to happen in our lives. If we had no way of knowing when we had to go to work, where we had to be on our days off and what was coming next, it would be very stressful for us. We would probably become short-tempered and angry.

For people with learning disabilities, especially people with autism, it is important for things to be predictable. People with learning disabilities may not have calendars or diaries to predict what is going to happen on a daily basis, so we may need to assist them with this.

We all have our own routines and ways we like to do things. Many of us like to park our cars in the same space or catch a train at a particular time. When we read the newspaper, we might start by reading the sports pages, television listings or horoscopes. We often rely on routine to help us get through the day. People with learning disabilities like routine, too. We can help people with learning disabilities with predictability, and routines can be used as part of this. Instead of using a diary, we can use a board with pictures on it to represent what will happen next. If someone has the same routine every day, they will start to know what is going to happen next and be less anxious about it.

Choice

Supporting people with learning disabilities to make choices is one of the most important aspects of our work. Being able to make our own choices is a fundamental right that we all have. When we deny people choices, it should not be a surprise that their behaviour becomes a challenge to us. Choices should range from day-to-day decisions, like what to wear or eat, to large decisions about where to work and live.

We need to present choices to people with learning disabilities in a way they can understand. We can use pictures or objects to demonstrate choices.

Some problems might arise, and these need to be considered. For example:

- The person may always say 'yes' to whatever they are offered, whether they like it or not. Or they may automatically say 'no' to whatever they are offered.
- The person may agree with the last thing that is offered. For example, if the support worker asks whether they would like cornflakes or toast for breakfast, they will reply 'toast', simply because it was the last thing in the list.

You can solve this by swapping the order in which you offer the choices or by asking open questions, instead of listing of choices.

Some people may become anxious when given a large list of choices, or they may have never been able to make choices for themselves before. We might need to limit choices initially, then build on this as the person becomes more accustomed to making choices.

We need to be imaginative, too. If the person does not understand what is being offered, we can use pictures or videos to help.

Often, the idea of choice is misunderstood. For example, someone may be left to lie in bed all day because the staff believe it is their choice to do so. If the person is not given the choice of any activity other than lying in bed, then that is not a choice.

Skills teaching

Teaching new skills to people with learning disabilities empowers them and makes them less dependent on members of staff. The less dependent they are on others, the less they may need to use behaviour that we find challenging. Task analysis is one popular method of skills teaching.

Task analysis

Skills can be taught by breaking tasks down into a series of steps. For example, when you wash your clothes, there are many steps involved. We can divide the task into chunks – putting the washing on, taking it out, drying it and so on. The steps for putting the washing on can be broken down as follows:

1. Gathering up the dirty washing
2. Separating light and dark colours
3. Carrying the washing to the machine
4. Opening the door
5. Putting the clothes in the machine
6. Closing the door
7. Putting the washing powder in the machine
8. Selecting the cycle you require
9. Switching the machine on

These nine distinct steps can be taught to someone so they can put their own washing on in future. An occupational therapist can help to draw up this sort of programme. Pictures, drawings or symbols to demonstrate each stage of the process could accompany the steps. A speech and language therapist can help with this.

The steps can be as small or broad as the person can understand, and you should try not to teach too many steps at one time. It is important that you do not miss out any steps and that you teach them in the right order.

Autism

Nobody knows exactly what causes autism, although there is some suggestion that it might be hereditary, and it is associated with some conditions that can cause learning disabilities.

Autism affects more men than women although, as the learning disability becomes more severe, more women are affected.

Having autism does not necessarily mean that the person's behaviour will be challenging, but the way people with autism interact with the world may make it more of a challenge for staff to meet their needs.

People with autism have three major difficulties that affect the way they interact with other people and their environment. These areas are:

- problems with communication
- problems with social interaction
- problems with the use of imagination, which leads to restricted, repetitive and stereotypic activities and behaviours.

There are other problems associated with autism, such as an oversensitivity to things like noise, touch or vision. People with autism may become irritated by strip lighting or too much noise, or might prefer not to wear certain clothes because they cannot bear the touch of them.

Communication

Staff may have to adapt the way they communicate with people with autism, and might not be able to take it for granted that the person will understand what they are saying by the way they say it or their body language.

Verbal communication

Many people with autism do not use verbal communication, and those who do may require a greater level of support to be understood. Those that are verbal might have an odd tone to their voice – they may speak in a very flat monotone, a high pitch or a strange accent. Some may talk in a very loud voice or a virtual whisper, even in places where it is not necessary or appropriate to do so.

Another communication difficulty people with autism might have is echolalia, where they echo the speech of others. They may immediately echo what someone has just said, or repeat it hours, days or even years later. This can cause problems if we assume the person is talking with us or understands exactly what we are saying.

People with autism tend to have a very literal understanding of the spoken word, and have trouble understanding metaphors. Expressions such as 'my mind is racing', 'jumping for joy' or 'he gets under my skin' are all metaphors. For the person with autism, the meaning can be lost or the phrase might be interpreted literally. For example, if someone asks you if you want to go for a drink, they're not asking you because they think you are thirsty, but this is how someone with autism might view it.

People with autism often have difficulty with the rules of spoken language. They may have problems starting a conversation, so might start one with an inappropriate phrase or by interrupting someone else's conversation. Once a conversation has started, they may have difficulty keeping the conversation going, or move from the original subject on to their favourite topic. They might talk at you rather than with you, showing little interest in what you are interested in and preferring to talk about their own subject.

People with autism may also invent their own words. These are called neologisms. This is where a person invents a word that has meaning for them. For example, someone may refer to a household object, such as a toothbrush, by a different name (see **Box 20: Examples of communication difficulties in people with autism**).

Box 20: Examples of communication difficulties in people with autism

Joan is a support worker and is having trouble helping one of the people she supports with their personal hygiene. The person has autism. The speech and language therapist listens to the way Joan interacts with the person, and notes that she uses terms like:

'Shall we have a bath?'
'You'd better shake a leg or you'll be late.'
'I'm going to run the bath.'
'Time is money.'
'Pull your socks up.'

When interpreted literally, none of these make much sense.

Martin echoes speech, and repeats the last words that are spoken to him. As a consequence, when he is offered a choice, he always appears to be choosing the last thing offered to him:

Support worker: 'Would you like tea or coffee?'
Martin: 'Coffee.'
Support worker: 'Do you want to go to the bowling alley or the cinema?'
Martin: 'Cinema.'

Julian wants to get the attention of a member of staff at the day centre, because he wants a drink. He approaches a member of staff and says, 'Do you like Elvis?'.

Jennie asks for a 'stirum' whenever she wants a cup of tea.

Parbatt talks in a very loud voice even when he is in a quiet restaurant, at college or in the library.

Non-verbal communication

People with autism also have problems understanding non-verbal communication. Much of what we say is conveyed in our posture, how close we stand to others, the gestures we use and our facial expressions. As support staff, we cannot assume that people with autism will be able to understand that we are joking because we are smiling, that we are saying no by shaking our head, or that we are in a relaxed or tense posture. When communicating, we must use very exact phrases and try not to rely on our body language to give extra information.

Box 21: Examples of non-verbal communication that may not be understood

- Raising your hand to your mouth to imitate drinking from a cup, to ask if someone wants a cup of tea.
- Shrugging your shoulders when you are asked what time dinner starts.
- Giving the thumbs-up sign to say 'yes' or 'good'.
- Winking to indicate that you are joking.

Imagination

People with autism have difficulties with imagination and this means they might have behaviours that they repeat or might be obsessed by a narrow area of interest or activities.

A lack of imagination can be seen in an inability to understand other people's feelings or abstract concepts like time or emotion. As a result, people with autism may spend a large amount of time engaged in routines or rituals that they *do* understand. They may have interests that take up a lot of their time or prevent them from being involved in other activities.

A lack of imagination can lead to the person becoming distressed when unexpected changes happen, such as changes in daily routine or changes in the environment the person is used to. When people with autism are under stress they are more likely to engage in stereotypic or ritualistic behaviour, as this is something they understand. They might have preferred ways of doing things, such as insisting on taking the familiar route to the shops.

People with autism can have difficulties transferring skills or knowledge from one area to another. If a parent points out a car to their child, they would expect their child to recognise other vehicles as being cars because they have the same attributes – four wheels, a similar shape and so on. A child with autism might only recognise other vehicles as cars if they are identical, so if the original car was a red Volkswagen Beetle the child will only recognise other red Volkswagen Beetles as cars. Someone who has been taught to make a cup of tea at the day centre might have trouble

Keeping it Together © Pavilion Publishing (Brighton) Ltd 2007

repeating this skill when they get home, because at home the kettle is a different shape, the sugar kept in a jar rather than a bowl, the cups a different colour and the milk in a jug rather than a bottle. All of these differences mean that the person might have to be re-taught to make a cup of tea in the new environment.

The person with autism may ask questions repeatedly, often when they know what the answer will be. Sometimes, they will only accept one answer and become upset if a different response is given.

They might hoard or collect often useless or bizarre objects, filling their room with what other people regard as rubbish. For example, they may collect spare parts from motorbikes, despite not owning a motorbike or knowing how to drive one.

There may be a fascination with parts of an object but a lack of concern with the whole object, for example, being interested in the television aerial rather than the picture on the screen. There may be a fascination with moving or spinning objects like rotating fans or spinning coins on a tabletop.

People with autism might engage in repetitive or obsessional touching of objects or people, sometimes in inappropriate situations or circumstances.

They may take up strange postures, hold their body in rigid positions or walk in strange ways such as in slow motion or on tiptoe. There may be other mannerisms, like flapping their hands in front of their eyes.

A lack of imagination can cause problems with understanding emotions like love, joy or hate. Other problems can occur around the concept of time and imagining the future, so it may be difficult for the person to understand ideas such as 'in four weeks time', 'next year' or 'tomorrow'.

Box 22: Examples of routines, rituals or mannerisms that may be seen in people with autism

- Mary will only cross the threshold from one room to another if she is walking backwards.

- Simon has to slowly count to one hundred every morning before getting out of bed.

- Leo will stand in the corridor flicking the light switch, watching the lights go on and off, for long periods of time.

- Roger will take the batteries out of all of the appliances, remote controls and clocks in the house and put them under his pillow.

- Eddie repetitively asks who will be on duty for the afternoon shift, even though he has been told several times already.

- Carmen will sit at the dining room table waving her fingers in front of her face for long periods of time.

- Whenever Susan goes into the bathroom, she arranges the bottles of shampoo, bars of soap, tubes of toothpaste and toilet cleaner in a straight line in the bath.

- Evander will spin the lid of the coffee jar round and round on the kitchen counter.

- Karl has kept every bus ticket he has ever been given. When he sees a bus ticket on the floor or in a bin, he picks it up and adds it to his large collection.

- Chris gets upset when a new member of staff uses a different route when taking him to the day centre.

- Raj started to self-injure when the front room of his house was decorated and the furniture was moved around.

We stressed earlier that you should not make threats to punish people with learning disabilities, as a way of reducing challenging behaviour. Because of their impairment in imagination, people with autism find it difficult to understand a threat (see *Box 23: Imagination example*).

Box 23: Imagination example

Paul has autism and attends a busy day service for people with learning disabilities. Paul often spends long periods of time in the toilet cubical, repeatedly flushing the toilet, rather than joining in the activities. The staff threaten Paul that if he stays in the toilet he will not be allowed to go horse riding on Friday. Their threats have not altered Paul's behaviour, so they ask members of the multi-disciplinary team to help.

The speech and language therapist points out that, due to impairments in his imagination, Paul probably cannot understand an abstract concept like 'next Friday' so will not be able to make a link between his behaviour now and something that will be happening later in the week.

The occupational therapist suggests that he spends a long time in the toilet because he does not know what activity or event is happening next. As a result, he becomes anxious and goes to the toilet where he carries out stereotypic behaviours. The occupational therapist also points out that the toilet is a low stimulation environment (less noise and activity), whereas the day centre can be very hectic.

To help with this problem, the staff team design a large board to which they can attach pictures with Velcro, to indicate what activity is coming next. As the day progresses, the pictures are moved along and activities that have passed are removed. Instead of threatening Paul, the staff direct him to the board when he arrives and as each activity starts and finishes.

Over the following months, more pictures are added to show Paul which staff are on duty and who will be co-ordinating each activity.

Paul begins to spend less time in the toilet, as he is not as anxious about what is going to happen next.

Theory of mind

Theory of mind is our ability to guess what is on the mind of others. We can usually work out why someone is behaving in a particular way because we can draw on our own experiences and we tend to know how people think. People with autism rarely develop this skill. For example, when someone asks us what we think of their new haircut, we would probably be polite and say that it looks nice. Asked the same question, someone with autism may well be brutally honest, not understanding that their comments may hurt someone's feelings.

People who have not developed theory of mind may also assume that other people know what they know (see *Box 24: Theory of mind*).

Box 24: Theory of mind

Peter is a man with autism who lives in a group home. Peter is obsessed with sport, and records any sporting events on television while he is at college.

Peter is in his bedroom trying to set his video recorder, but the video recorder is not working. Peter becomes increasingly frustrated because his video does not work. He eventually gets up and walks up to the first member of staff and screams at them, 'Why haven't you been helping me?'.

In this example, Peter assumes the staff member automatically knows that he is having a problem. This is because Peter believes that the member of staff knows exactly what he knows, and does not understand why they have not come to his assistance.

Social interaction

People with autism do not interact with others in the same way as people without autism. We have already discussed difficulties with communication, such as misunderstanding facial expressions, unusual eye contact and not following gestures, which can lead to problems. The problems that people with autism have in understanding people's feelings can also make them appear cold and disinterested in others.

Some of the problems around social interaction

Some people with autism may have difficulties in developing interpersonal relationships, especially with their peers. They might not make friends and when they do, they may have trouble with turn taking (for example, letting others speak). They may not share interests or activities with other people. They might not learn to imitate other people in a social way. They may show a lack of body language or facial expression in response to what others are saying.

Problems can also occur because people with autism have difficulty in understanding other people's feelings. We use these abilities to build trust and rapport or show our concern to others. For example, when someone tells you bad news, you expect their facial expression to show concern or sadness.

People with autism might not seek physical comfort in others, preferring not to hug other people or being indifferent to contact with them. They may not like to be touched.

People with autism may not realise that you can do things in one environment that are unacceptable in another. For example, you would not dress the same way to go to bed as you would to play a game of tennis.

How to support someone with autism

There are a number of things that can be done to support a person with autism. Each of the areas that they have difficulties with will need to be addressed.

- Limit your speech to saying exactly what needs to be done.

- Do not expect the person with autism to understand jokes, sarcasm or metaphor, and do not use these when speaking to them.

- Keep sentences short.

- Do not include too many keywords per sentence.

- Do not use negatives like 'can't', 'won't' or 'isn't'.

- Try to keep things concrete. Do not use abstract concepts – the person may not understand if you say 'later'.

- Remember that the person might not understand body language or facial expressions. Do not expect facial expressions or body language to accompany or reflect the speech of people with autism.

- The person's speech might be an echo of what they have heard before, rather than conversation.

- Provide a visual planner so the person with autism can see what will happen in the future.

- Don't expect the person's skills to be generalised – because they learned to do something in one environment, it does not mean they will be able to carry out the same skill elsewhere.

- Remember that, when someone with autism is anxious or does not understand what is happening next, they may revert to ritualistic behaviour.

- Try not to make unnecessary changes in activities and routines.

- Remember that the person with autism may assume that you know what they know.

- Bear in mind that the person is likely to have difficulty understanding your or others' feelings.

- There may be a problem with sensory stimulation. Be aware that noises, clashing colours and strip lighting may cause discomfort.

section five

Working in the long term

So far, we have talked about what challenging behaviour is and why it might happen. We have looked at what we might do to react when faced with challenging behaviour. This section looks at what we can do in the long term to make permanent changes, and how various professionals can help with this.

Assessment

As we said earlier, challenging behaviour can often be seen as a form of communication. ***Box 25: Using self-injurious behaviour to communicate needs*** gives four examples to show how someone might use self-injurious behaviour to communicate their needs. The assessment process will examine what the person might be 'trying to say' so that we can find alternative ways for them to say it.

Box 25: Using self-injurious behaviour to communicate needs

Example	What someone with a learning disability might be thinking	What might happen
Althea is helping to mop the floor but doesn't understand the task properly, so she begins to bite her hand.	'I want this to stop because I don't understand what is going on.'	A member of staff thinks that Althea is distressed, asks her to stop mopping the floor and asks her to do another activity.
Bill has been sitting in his wheelchair on his own in the lounge for two hours. He begins to poke himself in the eye, which he finds stimulating.	'I was bored, but this is more interesting.'	A member of staff sees this and wheels Bill to the kitchen where he can help prepare the dinner. (It may seem strange that someone might want to poke themselves in the eye for something to do, but for someone who does not have much going on or other means of entertainment, this might be the case.)
Julian is unoccupied. He sees a member of staff walk by and rocks violently in the armchair so that his head hits the wall.	'I'm bored and want to spend some time with someone.'	The member of staff comes over, tells Julian to stop and puts their hand on his shoulder to comfort him.
Lisa is sitting in the lounge. She can smell food cooking in the kitchen. She starts to slap herself in the face.	'I want something to eat.'	A member of staff sees Lisa slapping her face and guesses that she wants something to eat.

Gathering information might help us to understand the reason why someone has behaviour that we find challenging. Once we know the reason, specialists and staff can come up with ideas to help the individual to learn other behaviours.

The ABC chart

The most common and best-known assessment tool is the Antecedent, Behaviour, Consequence (ABC) chart. This seeks to find out what is going on around the individual when there is challenging behaviour.

- A (Antecedent) – what was going on before the behaviour occurred
- B (Behaviour) – what the challenging behaviour was
- C (Consequence) – what happened afterwards

Specialists working in challenging behaviour or your manager may want you to complete a lot of ABC charts.

Earlier, we talked about how challenging behaviour can result from learned behaviour. The ABC chart can tell us why it happens (see the example in ***Box 26: The ABC chart***).

Box 26: The ABC chart

Antecedent:	Jim has been left unoccupied in a wheelchair in the living room of his home for the past two hours.
Behaviour:	Another person living there, Sabri, walks past. Jim leans across and grabs his arm, which makes Sabri scream.
Consequence:	The staff run to Jim and tell him to loosen his grip, then wheel him into the dining room where the staff are having a meeting.

Someone looking at the example in ***Box 26: The ABC chart*** might think that Jim was bored because he had been left alone for hours. By hurting another person, his boredom stops because he has learned over the years that staff have to do something when he hurts someone – they may tell him off or take him somewhere more interesting.

Problems in completing ABC charts

A common problem with ABC charts is that they are not completed properly. ***Box 27a: Jim (a)*** and ***Box 27b: Jim (b)*** show how different people might interpret the example of Jim from ***Box 26: The ABC chart*** that we have just looked at.

Box 27a: Jim (a)

Antecedent:	Jim was watching the television in the living room.
Behaviour:	Jim became aggressive toward Sabri.
Consequence:	The staff moved Jim out of the living room.

Note: This account does not mention the time that Jim had spent with nothing to do, the type of aggression he displayed or what happened to Jim other than that he left the living room.

Box 27b: Jim (b)

Antecedent:	Jim was in the living room, watching a boxing match on television. The boxing match made him feel violent.
Behaviour:	Jim grabbed Sabri.
Consequence:	The staff moved Jim away from the television as it was getting him worked up.

*Note: This account describes what the person reporting thought Jim **felt** – not what the person actually observed happening.*

A lot of ABC charts will have to be filled in before the reason for the person behaving in a certain way is really understood.

Tick boxes

Instead of an ABC chart, you might be asked to fill in a tick box to record behaviour. A tick box may be able to tell us at what time of day, or where, a behaviour is happening.

Specialists

As well as examining the behaviour, we need to consider what is going on for the individual. Earlier, we said that challenging behaviour might arise from a lack of activities, or from being dependent on others. A specialist might ask staff what is going on in the person's life, to see if this might be affecting their behaviour. They might ask questions like, 'When is the behaviour most likely to occur?' or 'What activities does the person do?'. The specialist might use interviews with staff, observations of the individual or rating scales to ask the questions (see *Box 28: Information that specialists might want to know*).

Box 28: Information that specialists might want to know

Specialists might want to know the following information about the person whose behaviour is challenging:

- past referrals to specialists. This way, the specialist can see if there is an ongoing problem and what help has been given in the past

- what medicines the person has been given in the past and what they are taking now

- guidelines – how the challenging behaviour is being dealt with at present and what ideas were used in the past; did these ideas work in the past, what bits did not work?

- health and medical aspects of the person's life (i.e. epilepsy, syndromes, illnesses or hearing problems)

- communication skills – how the person communicates. Challenging behaviour may be due to communication difficulties, so this is very important

- previous incident reports. These can provide information on when, where and why a behaviour may have occurred

- staff opinions – for example, on why you believe the behaviour occurs

- the person's strengths and needs. Strengths can be built on and support can be found for the individual's needs

- daily activities – how the person spends their time. A lack of activities may be what is causing the challenging behaviour

- what the person enjoys doing, what their preferred activities are – not just the negative aspects of the person's life

- any recent changes that may have upset the individual (e.g. staff changes, bereavement, altered routines).

Some of this information could be gathered in advance before a specialist comes to assess. This will help with assessment and help you to look at areas you may not have considered before.

Long-term interventions

 Staff are constantly reacting to problems and not being proactive.

Quote from a challenging needs practitioner

When the specialist has gathered enough information, they will give you ideas for interventions that might help. Interventions can be divided into what to do immediately – when the challenging behaviour is happening – and what you can do in the long term. Long-term interventions will have come from the results of the assessment and will be specific to the individual's needs. They are designed to reduce or remove the challenging behaviour, and replace it with more appropriate behaviours.

We covered immediate interventions when we discussed reactive strategies on pages 12–16. In this section, we will be looking at long-term interventions.

Long-term interventions should be aimed at increasing inclusion, choice and relationships for the individual. For example, someone whose behaviour is challenging may not go out as much because they need extra staff to accompany them, or there may be places they cannot go because of their behaviour. A lack of inclusion, as well as limited choice, respect and social networks could be why the person you are supporting was challenging in the first place. Interventions that improve these areas should have a positive affect on an individual's behaviour and lead to a better quality of life (see ***Box 29: Diagram of the vicious cycle of challenging behaviour***).

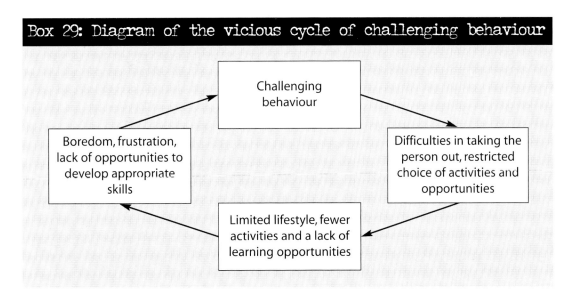

Box 29: Diagram of the vicious cycle of challenging behaviour

When activities are considered, we need to make sure that they are appropriate to that individual's level of ability, and that they want to do them. If an activity is too difficult or the person dislikes it, it is unlikely to be of any help.

Long-term interventions will build on the person's existing skills rather than just looking to reduce an unwanted behaviour. If a challenging behaviour is the only way someone has any control over the world around them, it could be considered unethical to attempt to take that away. This is one reason why we try to replace behaviours that are challenging with appropriate ones.

By teaching someone you support a new way of behaving in a situation, they will not have to rely on the use of challenging behaviour (see **Box 30: Demonstrating how new appropriate behaviours can replace challenging behaviours**).

Box 30: Demonstrating how new appropriate behaviours can replace challenging behaviours		
Challenging behaviour	**New behaviour**	**How staff and specialists work together to do this**
Simon would bang his head during cookery at college when he couldn't cope with the session any more.	Simon was taught the Makaton sign for 'break'. He can now use this sign whenever he has had enough.	Speech and language therapy assessed Simon and encouraged staff to use the 'break' sign with Simon whenever he was given time away from a task. He began to associate the sign for break with having time away from a task. Whenever Simon used the sign, this was reinforced by his receiving a break and being praised by staff.
Sarah would pinch the other residents whenever she was bored at home, in order to get a reaction out of them.	Sarah was taught to show a member of staff a video cassette to indicate she wanted to watch a film. Over time, Sarah was taught to use the video machine whenever she wanted to watch a film.	Before a video was put on, staff showed Sarah the video cassette so that she began to associate the video with watching a film. Whenever Sarah showed staff the cassette, she received encouragement and the film was put on for her to watch. Staff taught Sarah to use the video player by putting a brightly coloured sticker on the play button; other stickers were introduced for other functions on the video player.
Karl would go into the kitchen and scream when he wanted a drink. Eventually, the staff would make him a drink and his screaming would stop.	Karl was shown a laminated picture of a cup of tea every time he was given a drink. In time, he associated the picture with getting a cup of tea and would present it to staff to indicate his needs. Now staff can assist him to make a drink, until he has learned to do it independently.	Speech and language therapy assessed Karl's ability to understand photographs and symbols. When Karl started to scream in the kitchen, he was shown the laminated picture and assisted to make tea.

The examples in *Box 30: Demonstrating how new appropriate behaviours can replace challenging behaviours* show how, once we have found out why somebody is doing something, we can support the person to develop new behaviours that are not challenging, and improve their quality of life. *Box 31: Other examples of interventions to help people whose behaviour is challenging* briefly shows how challenging behaviour can be decreased by teaching new skills, changing how staff interact or offering activities.

Box 31: Other examples of interventions to help people whose behaviour is challenging

- John is taught to use a stress-ball instead of pulling at his hair when he is feeling nervous.

- Simon used to lose his temper quickly. He went to anger management classes, and was then able to do relaxation exercises whenever he felt himself getting tense.

- Mary has trouble understanding what comes next in the day and in what sequence her activities run. A picture timetable helps her to understand.

- Using sign language or pictures to accompany speech helps George, who has communication difficulties.

- Vicki often becomes aggressive because she doesn't understand why she is being asked to polish the tables. By changing her daily activity from polishing to making lunch, it becomes more meaningful for her, as she can eat her sandwich when she has made it.

- Ian self-injures if he is left unoccupied for long periods. Staff rarely have time to work with Ian individually, because of the time they spend cleaning, doing laundry and cooking. A psychologist suggested that Ian should be included in the household chores and an occupational therapist helped advise what methods to use. Ian is now occupied in meaningful activities whenever he wants, by assisting in the running of his own house.

- Staff often have difficulty thinking of new activities and are unsure about what the people they support did during the previous shift. A plan of activities and a recording sheet help staff to find meaningful activities that are not repetitive.

- Barbara is often left out of household activities because she has difficulty concentrating for long periods and will wander away before completing a task. The occupational therapist suggests that Barbara is still involved, even if she is only involved for a few minutes. The staff now encourage Barbara to participate for short periods and prompt her to return when she has had a sufficient break.

- Jerome was considered unable to join in with preparing food because he has trouble co-ordinating his hands. The staff team found that he could still join in if they helped him to stir or chop by holding his hand in theirs. The staff found that Jerome could enjoy a number of leisure and work activities by doing this.

- Jasmine would become anxious when she encountered new situations and would begin to bite her lip. Staff practised ways to behave with Jasmine and things to say to her in these situations, to prepare her for the future.

❝ *It can be a long process and not something that is achieved overnight.* ❞

Quote from challenging needs worker

Once interventions have been set up, it is the job of the support staff to carry them out. Managers of supported houses need to ensure that all the staff are doing this in the same way (see **Box 32: Beverly**).

Box 32: Beverly

Beverly has moderate learning disabilities and behaviour that challenges, and lives in a small supported house.

The staff team have contacted the challenging behaviour team because Beverley will strip off her clothes when she has been left without an activity for a while.

After doing an assessment, the challenging behaviour team gather together the staff team, and explain why Beverley is behaving this way. They also present a plan to help with this.

The challenging behaviour team have designed a programme. Part of this involves Beverly receiving a sticker every time she asks for staff attention in an appropriate manner. Whenever Beverly behaves appropriately, she receives a sticker that goes on a chart. When the chart has ten stickers on it, Beverley is supported to buy a new CD, as she enjoys music. The money to pay for the CD is provided by the service that runs Beverly's house.

The programme begins but some of the staff don't feel that Beverley will understand what the stickers mean, so do not bother to follow it through. Others are annoyed because it means extra work.

The challenging behaviour team return two weeks later and find that the programme has not been a success. The staff have a team meeting to discuss why. Some of the staff team had believed that the challenging behaviour team would be working with Beverley – not them. Others had thought that the challenging behaviour team would prescribe medication or take Beverley away for a few hours a day so they could have a break.

Note: When a programme is designed like this, the individual's own money should not be used to fund it. Professionals should always be involved to ensure that the programme is ethical and that it is designed correctly.

Organising the service – staff support, team work, planning, reviewing

Organisation within the house is necessary when dealing with challenging behaviour. Interventions need to be adhered to consistently. This can be helped by planning in advance (see **Box 33: Good practice in interventions**).

Box 33: Good practice in interventions

Staff from challenging behaviour teams give the following examples of good practice that have helped in interventions:

- good induction, training, guidance and support for new staff
- good role models, mentors and supervision for junior staff
- staff who understand that their job role includes teaching the people they support and carrying out behavioural support programmes – not just cleaning, cooking and balancing the petty cash
- managers who take responsibility for interventions working
- having a staff team who realise who is meant to be doing what
- support workers who know they should fill in forms, and that forms are not just a job for managers
- services in which there are documents and these are available and read by all members of staff
- clear recording systems that are easy to understand
- services that do not rely too much on bank or agency staff
- services that have low staff turnover
- services that have regular discussions and house meetings
- staff being allowed to go on a variety of training courses.

Using external professionals

When they are faced with challenging behaviour, it is likely that staff teams will need to make referrals to specialists. A referral is usually made through the community learning disability team. A form will probably need to be filled in and posted off.

Most community learning disability teams have waiting lists and you may have to wait before a professional can see the person you are referring. You may need to make referrals to more than one group of professionals, such as psychologists, a challenging behaviour team, speech and language therapists, psychiatrists or occupational therapists.

When a referral has gone through, a specialist will want to meet with the individual whose behaviour is challenging and one or more members of staff. It is helpful if time is put aside for a meeting, and that the person attending the meeting is supernumerary for that shift.

Working with a challenging behaviour team or psychologist – what they can do

Challenging behaviour teams are made up of psychologists or people who have done specialist training in challenging behaviour. As we have discussed throughout this section, they will assess someone's behaviour and develop interventions based on their assessment. Do not expect one of these specialists to be able to turn up and solve problems overnight. Any interventions that they suggest will have to be carried out by the staff team working with the individual.

Working with speech and language therapists – what they can do

As discussed earlier, challenging behaviour often has its origins in difficulties with communication. Difficulties might lie in the person's ability to make themselves understood to others or their ability to understand what other people are trying to say to them.

Speech and language therapists can carry out assessments of someone's communication needs, both verbal and non-verbal. For example, they may be able to assess how much information someone can understand at one time. Staff can then adapt the way they communicate to a level the person can understand.

A speech and language therapist may also be able to teach non-verbal forms of communication, such as adapted sign languages like Makaton or Signalong. They may be able to suggest objects, pictures, photographs or symbols that the individual can use to communicate.

Working with occupational therapists – what they can do

People whose behaviour is a challenge may rely on other people to have their needs met. This can lead to dependency. If someone has behaviour we find a challenge, they may not be offered as many activities as other people. This may lead to a lack of choice, inclusion and stimulation. Being dependent on others and having a lack of stimulating things to do might result in challenging behaviour (see *Box 26: The ABC chart*).

If someone is taught new skills, they will be less reliant on others. This may help in reducing the behaviour that we find challenging.

Occupational therapists might be able to help staff to teach new skills to someone they support, or give suggestions for more activities for the individual.

An occupational therapist may also be able to provide information on environmental factors that might be contributing to challenging behaviour, and to draw up guidelines to help change the environment around the person. They may be able to provide adaptations, aids or utensils to help the individual.

Working with psychiatrists, general practitioners (GPs) and nurses – what they can do

A psychiatrist is a doctor who specialises in treating people with mental health problems. A psychiatrist's role is to assess, diagnose, manage and treat mental health problems. A psychiatrist might prescribe medicines.

A general practitioner (GP) is most people's first port of call if they have a health problem. The GP can then refer the person on to a specialist service if they feel that it is needed.

Someone you support might have a learning disability nurse. These nurses specialise in working with people with learning disabilities. They develop care plans to help meet the health needs of people with learning disabilities. Some nurses may have done additional training in challenging behaviour or mental health, and work in these areas as their speciality.

Use of medication

In certain circumstances, medication can be prescribed for challenging behaviour. This is typically a short-term measure until appropriate interventions can be put in place, at which point the medication should no longer be needed.

In a small number of cases, such as mental health problems, medication might be needed in the long term. People with mental health problems, with and without learning disabilities, may benefit from the use of medication. People with learning disabilities can develop mental health problems, just as people without learning disabilities can. If the individual has a mental health problem, then they may be prescribed a medication to help with that particular illness. This should only be done after a thorough assessment, usually by a qualified psychiatrist, or occasionally the person's GP if it is a mild mental health problem.

Staff often assume that challenging behaviour is due to a mental health problem. Some mental health problems might result in an increase in challenging behaviour but, often, challenging behaviour is caused by environmental factors that can be changed.

When medication is prescribed because of challenging behaviour, it should be as part of the care plan and not as a substitute for psychological or behavioural interventions. The lowest efficient dose possible should be used, and only when the perceived benefits are not outweighed by the negative side effects of taking the medication. The person's behaviour should be monitored to check that the medication is having an effect, and it should be withdrawn if there is no apparent benefit. All efforts should continue to be made to find out why the person's behaviour is challenging.

PRN medication guidelines

PRN is short for the Latin *pro re nata* meaning 'as needed'. When medication is prescribed on an 'as needed' basis, the prescriber should specify when it is appropriate to give the medication. For example, it might only be used when someone is aggressive or self-injuring, after all other attempts to calm the individual have failed and the individual or others are at risk.

We need to remember that when we give medication to someone who is aggressive we are not 'curing' the problem that is making them aggressive; we are just not having to deal with the behaviour for a few hours. So we should not become reliant on giving PRN medication whenever we feel challenged.

When staff are expected to give PRN medication, there need to be clear guidelines about its use. The guidelines should indicate:

- when the PRN medication should be used (for example, if someone is self-injuring, do you give the medication after five minutes of continuous self-injury, half an hour of intermittent self-injury etc.)

- what size of dose to give and at what frequency this can be repeated

- what side-effects to look out for

- whether staff should be aware that the medicated individual may have impaired performance while under the influence of the medication

- whether the individual has consented to PRN medication

- a set timeframe for review – PRN medication should not be used in the long term; if it is being used too frequently, a review will be needed to identify why this is happening.

Behavioural programmes

Interventions designed for people with learning disabilities usually involve changing the way the service works for the individual, for example, by improving their quality of life by offering more choices and activities, or by increasing their skills. Advice may be given on how staff can interact or communicate with the individual.

In rarer cases, behavioural interventions may be introduced when the individual or those around them are at risk. One of the most common methods is to give the person something every time they behave in a way that is appropriate. This will mean that they use the behaviour that we find a challenge less often. Behavioural interventions should only be drawn up by qualified professionals. They should always explain to your staff team why they have come up with this programme.

section six

What people with learning disabilities think

In **Section One: Facing challenging behaviour for the first time**, we discussed what challenging behaviour is. People with learning disabilities have their own thoughts and feelings about what challenging behaviour means to them. In developing this guide, we interviewed a number of people with learning disabilities for their opinions about challenging behaviour. As well as aggressive acts, they also felt that challenging behaviour could mean people bullying you, calling you names or being rude. People with learning disabilities' views are shown on page 72.

They identified the behaviour of other people with whom they live, go to college and attend day centres. They also said that the behaviour of some of the staff they work with can be challenging, too.

They said that staff can be challenging when they:

- tell you off
- are rude
- are being too bossy
- discriminate
- criticise
- use terms like 'mental handicap'
- are too nosy.

As staff, we have to consider our own actions and how these can contribute to challenging behaviour.

❝ Sometimes it's the staff that are challenging – when they tell you off or get bossy. ❞

Quote from a man with a learning disability

People with learning disabilities were asked how challenging behaviour makes them feel and they said that they felt nervous, scared and upset, but also wanted to shout or scream back at the person who had upset them. Although they had angry feelings, they understood that it may not be the person's fault and that they needed help.

They felt that some of the reasons that challenging behaviour existed were a result of people with learning disabilities having nothing to do, having to stay indoors all the time or watching too much television. Having nothing to do could lead to frustration. They also felt that the staff not listening, or shouting and being rude might contribute to challenging behaviour.

❝ I sometimes get scared and nervous. ❞

Quote from a woman with a learning disability

People with learning disabilities felt that there were a number of things that the staff could do when someone's behaviour became challenging. None of them felt that the person should be punished. Instead, they suggested that staff could:

- sit down with the person
- talk to them
- get them to calm down
- encourage them to take deep breaths
- take them for a walk
- try doing something different
- find out why they were becoming challenging.

❝ Staff need to find out why they have challenging behaviour. ❞

Quote from a man with a learning disability

They felt that the behaviour of people with learning disabilities was less likely to become challenging if:

- they had access to a counsellor, advocacy groups or a citizen advocate
- they had things to do in the daytime, like going to a day service; they felt that challenging behaviour was likely to increase in the summer when colleges shut and there was less to do
- they were not left to get bored

- they had a job
- they had something to look forward to
- they were asked about what they wanted to do.

They felt that the behaviour of people with severe learning disabilities might become challenging because:

- the staff are not patient enough with them
- they are not taken out very much
- they need to have things demonstrated or shown to them in order to learn
- they require respect and friendships just like everyone else
- they may not be able to tell people what they want, so staff need to use pictures or tapes to communicate
- they may be ill (for example, they might have epilepsy) and not be able to tell anyone about it.

They also said that, just because they have a severe learning disability it does not mean they cannot tell you what they want.

Conclusion

The people with learning disabilities that we interviewed were very astute in understanding challenging behaviour. Challenging behaviour upset them but they realised that there was a reason that it happened. They realised that the staff should be looking at why challenging behaviour happened and that it could be due to not having much to do or limited opportunities. They also felt that staff sometimes contributed to the challenging behaviour and that the ways that staff behaved could be challenging to the people they support.

appendix one

Glossary

ABC chart Antecedent, Behaviour, Consequence chart. A chart used to record what happened before and after a behaviour you are studying, to help you find out why someone is behaving in a particular way.

Autism A disorder that affects someone's whole life. There are difficulties with communication, imagination and interacting with people socially.

Appropriate behaviour Behaviour that is acceptable to all those involved.

Antecedent What happened before a behaviour that you are recording.

Backward chaining Teaching a task in a series of individual steps. The steps are taught in reverse order, starting with the completed task and working backwards.

Chaining Teaching a task in a series of individual steps.

Challenging behaviour Behaviour that is serious enough to prevent people from being able to go where they want and do what they want. Behaviour that staff find challenging.

Consistency When all members of staff work with someone they are supporting in exactly the same way.

Constructive approach Building on an individual's existing skills to learn new, appropriate behaviours rather than trying to get rid of behaviours you do not like.

Desensitisation	Step-by-step way of slowly introducing someone to something that makes him or her anxious. For example, if someone has a fear of spiders, they are first taught to relax then, as a first step, are shown a picture of a spider. For the next step, they might look at a spider in a jar. This would continue in small steps over a number of hours, days or weeks until they can cope with the thing that makes them anxious.
Hereditary	Something that is passed down through the family, via their genes.
Inclusion	People being involved in the running of their own lives and being members of the community.
Intervention	Procedures put into place that should help to reduce challenging behaviour or increase someone's quality of life.
Neologisms	'Made-up' words that have meaning to the person who invented them but no one else. Seen in autism and in mental health problems like schizophrenia.
PRN medication	PRN is an abbreviation of the Latin *pro re nata*, meaning 'when needed'. It means a medication that is prescribed to be taken when needed, so it is not given all of the time. Examples might be paracetamol for when someone is in pain, or sometimes drugs like lorazepam are used when people are agitated.
Psychologist	A professional who can help people with learning disabilities by helping with their behaviour and thoughts.
Reinforcer	Something that makes a behaviour happen more often or less often.
Ritualistic behaviour	Behaviour that the person does repeatedly. Others may not see it as having any purpose. It is sometimes called 'stereotypic behaviour'.
Supernumerary	When a member of staff is not counted in the number of staff needed to run the service for that day (i.e. an extra member of staff who is free to do other duties or a new member of staff who is learning how to do the job).
Unethical	An intervention that would not be morally right, or that would be against someone's human rights.

appendix two

Bibliography and resources

(All websites accessed 29 August 2006)

References

Baker P (2002) Confrontation or Communication?: Supporting people whose behaviour challenges us. In: S Carnaby (Ed) *Learning Disability Today*. Brighton: Pavilion Publishing.

Jones E, Perry J, Lowe K, Allen D, Toogood S & Felce D (1997) *Active Support: A Handbook for Planning Daily Activities and Support Arrangements for People with Learning Disabilities*. Welsh Centre for Learning Disabilities Applied Research Unit.

British Institute of Learning Disabilities (2006) *The BILD Code of Practice for the use of Physical Interventions* (2nd Edition).

Networks

Mental Health in Learning Disabilities Network
www.estiacentre.org
A free-to-join email network for anyone interested in the mental health needs of people with learning disabilities.

National Network for Learning Disability Nurses (NNLDN) and the Access to Acute Care Network

www.nnldn.org.uk

The NNLDN is a 'network of networks', which aims to support networks and nurses in the field of learning disabilities. The website contains lots of information on access to acute care services.

UK Health and Learning Disability Network

www.ldhealthnetwork.org.uk

A free-to-join email network for anyone with an interest in the health needs of people with learning disabilities.

The Choice Forum

Aims to bring together people working with people with learning disabilities to discuss a variety of topical issues and share information. To join, go to the **Foundation for People with Learning Disabilities** website at *www.learningdisabilities.org.uk*

Useful organisations

British Institute of Learning Disabilities (BILD)
Campion House
Green Street
Kidderminster
Worcestershire
DY10 1JL

Tel: 01562 723010
Fax: 01562 723029
Web: www.bild.org.uk

BILD provides research and training on a wide range of issues affecting people with learning disabilities and has a range of free leaflets to download and publications/training materials to purchase.

Disability Rights Commission
DRC
FREEPOST MID02164
Stratford upon Avon
CV37 9BR

Tel: 08457 622 633
Fax: 08457 778 878
Web: www.drc.org.uk

National organisation that fights for a society in which all disabled people can participate fully as equal citizens.

Down's Syndrome Association

Langdon Down Centre
2a Langdon Park
Teddington
TW11 9PS

Tel: 0845 230 0372
Fax: 0845 230 0373
Email: info@downs-syndrome.org.uk
Web: www.dsa-uk.com

This organisation helps people with Down's syndrome to live full and rewarding lives. It provides a range of downloadable information.

The Elfrida Society

34 Islington Park Street
London
N1 1PX

Tel: 020 7359 7443
Email: elfrida@elfrida.com
Web: www.elfrida.com

The Elfrida Society researches better ways of supporting people with learning disabilities and provides a wide range of accessible information on health issues.

Estia Centre

66 Snowsfields
London
SE1 3SS

Tel: 020 7378 3217/8
Fax: 020 7378 3223
Email: estia@kcl.ac.uk
Web: www.estiacentre.org

Specialises in the mental health needs of people with learning disabilities, and provides training, research and development. Has a number of downloadable resources.

Foundation for People with Learning Disabilities

9th Floor
Sea Containers House
20 Upper Ground
London
SE1 9QB

Tel: 020 7803 1100
Fax: 020 7803 1111
Email: fpld@fpld.org.uk
Web: www.learningdisabilities.org.uk

National organisation that promotes the rights, quality of life and opportunities for people with learning disabilities through research, development and influencing policy. Free resources to download and purchase.

Mencap

123 Golden Lane
London
EC1Y 0RT

Tel: 020 7454 0454
Fax: 020 7696 5540
Email: information@mencap.org.uk
Web: www.mencap.org.uk

National organisation that fights for equal rights and greater opportunities for people with learning disabilities.

National Autistic Society

393 City Road
London
EC1V 1NG

Tel: 020 7833 2299
Fax: 020 7833 9666
Email: nas@nas.org.uk
Web: www.nas.org.uk

National organisation that fights for the rights and interests of all people with autism to ensure that they and their families receive quality services appropriate to their needs. Produces a number of free leaflets and publications/training materials for purchase.

Royal National Institute for the Blind (RNIB)

105 Judd Street
London
WC1H 9NE

Tel: 020 7388 1266
Fax: 020 7388 2034
Email: helpline@rnib.org.uk
Web: www.rnib.org.uk

Offers information, support and advice to more than two million people with sight problems.

Royal National Institute for the Deaf (RNID)

19–23 Featherstone Street
London
EC1Y 8SL

Tel: 0808 808 0123
Fax: 0808 808 9000
Email: information@rnid.org.uk
Web: www.rnid.org.uk

Offers information, support and advice to more than two million people with hearing problems.

The Tizard Centre

University of Kent at Canterbury

Canterbury

CT2 7LZ

Tel: 01227 764000

Web: www.kent.ac.uk/tizard

Training, research and development centre, which specialises in challenging behaviour.

Useful websites

Ask Mencap

www.askmencap.info

Provides lots of downloadable information on issues relevant to people with learning disabilities and their carers.

Challenging Behaviour Foundation

www.thecbf.org.uk

Provides guidance and information on supporting people whose behaviour is challenging, including downloadable fact sheets.

Contact a Family

www.cafamily.org.uk

Provides information on the health needs and syndromes associated with children with disabilities.

Easy Info (how to make information accessible)

http.easyinfo.org.uk

Provides guidance on how to make information accessible.

The Fragile X Society

www.fragilex.org.uk

Advice and information about the needs of people with fragile X syndrome.

Intellectual disability health information

www.intellectualdisability.info

Provides a wealth of information on the health needs of people with learning disabilities.

Mencap's guidance on making information accessible

www.mencap.org.uk/html/accessibility/accessibility_guides.htm

Guidance on how to make information accessible.

People First

www.peoplefirstltd.com

A national self-advocacy organisation run by people with learning difficulties for people with learning difficulties.

Prader-Willi Syndrome Association UK

http://pwsa.co.uk

Organisation offering advice, support and information on Prader-Willi syndrome.

Scope

www.scope.org.uk

Promotes equal rights and improved quality of life for disabled people, especially those with cerebral palsy.

Tuberous Sclerosis Association

www.tuberous-sclerosis.org

Supports sufferers, promotes awareness, and seeks the causes and best possible management of tuberous sclerosis.

Turner's Syndrome Support Society

www.tss.org.uk

Support and information for girls and adult women with Turner syndrome, their families and friends.

Valuing People Support Team

www.valuingpeople.gov.uk

Government agency that supports the implementation of *Valuing People*.

appendix three

Example of a risk management tool

Page 1

Reason for risk assessment – what is/are the risk(s)?

This is where you write what the risk is.

What are the positives in taking this risk or letting this situation continue?

This is where you write why you think you should take this risk - all the good things that should result from taking the risk.

What are the negative consequences of taking this risk? What might happen if this risk is not managed?

In this box, enter all the negative things that might result from taking the risk (for example, any harm, embarrassment, misunderstanding or danger that might come out of taking the risk).

What factors might influence risk?

There are many things that might either make risk-taking more successful or increase the danger. For example, does the individual have behaviour that is challenging, autism or communication problems? Do they prefer staff they have worked with for a long time?

84

Who should be invited to the risk management meeting

Name	Relationship/role/designation/profession
Enter the names of the people that have an interest in the risk process (i.e. advocates, staff, friends, family, members of the MDT and, of course, the individual with a learning disability themselves).	

What triggers are there to the person coming to harm, or situations in which that is more likely to happen?

Enter any situations in which, or times when, the person is more likely to come to harm.

What historical information might help indicate a potential risk?

Any information from the person's past can be put in this box.

Any other relevant information?

If there is any other information that may influence the risk management, this should be entered in this box.

Page 3

Management plan

The action plan to reduce the risk from happening (what, how, who, when?)

Enter in this box your ideas to reduce the risk.

What is the contingency plan in the event of the risk still happening?

Enter in this box what to do if there are problems (i.e. making sure a member of staff is carrying a mobile phone, ID cards, money etc.).

Long-term strategies to reduce risk (anger management, skills teaching, etc.)

These will not reduce the risk immediately, but may help over a period of weeks or months.

What strengths does the individual have that might work as a resource to support the risk management plan?

The person with learning disabilities may have preferences or abilities that can help when designing your risk management plan.

Any staffing issues or preferred staff to carry out management plan?

Initially, it may be wise to use experienced staff or those that the person with learning disabilities knows well, until the risk has minimised.

Date of next meeting/review

Risk management should be an ongoing process, with reviews.